This work is dedicated to Dr. Mario Rivera of San Juan, Puerto Rico, the founder of the Theotherapy method of ministry. The principles contained in this book are based upon his teachings...without his efforts and inspiration the Theotherapy Project would not exist.

A Brief History of Theotherapy

The model of ministry known as Theotherapy was developed in the early 1960's by Dr. Mario Rivera Mendez of San Juan, Puerto Rico. Dr. Rivera received degrees in psychology, theology and physical therapy and then utilized his knowledge in each of these areas to develop a ministry that positively affects the intellect, emotions and will of individuals. The Theotherapy model has an eclectic approach to ministry and utilizes biblical principles of emotional healing as well as many of the principles contained in counseling and psychology. The principles he developed are in use all over the world. This book is based upon his teachings and is dedicated to him.

The ministry of Theotherapy was further developed in the United States by Luena Darr, Executive Director of Theotherapy Seminars, Incorporated, who established Theotherapy centers in Pennsylvania, Ohio, Tennessee, North Carolina and Texas. She dedicates her time and vast knowledge to the training of new leaders in the Theotherapy model.

The Theotherapy Project was established by Mark and Dana West, students of Dr. Rivera and Luena Darr. Struck by the impact of the Theotherapy ministry model in their own lives and marriage, Mark and Dana saw how the principles of Theotherapy could effectively change the lives of those whom society has been compelled to incarcerate because of crime, violence and abusive behaviors. Their vision to reach incarcerated individuals with the healing principles of Theotherapy led to the establishment of Theotherapy Project initiatives in several Tennessee prisons and the writing of this book.

While not primarily a self-help book, this material is best used in small group settings and discussion forums and is an excellent discipleship tool. For more information on Theotherapy call (615)-525-3841 or visit us on the web at www.theotherapyproject.com.

All proceeds from the sale of this book go to support the continuing work of Theotherapy.

Contents

Introduction
The Pilgrimage of Healing

In the late 1990's I had the privilege of going to the nation of Israel to do some music for a couple of youth leadership conferences where American evangelical teens and Israeli teens partnered together for a week of topical lectures and historical site seeing. The goal of the conference was to help these young men and women brainstorm ideas and to reflect on the similarities and differences in cultural, societal and generational issues that affect teenagers of all nationalities. Other than getting to fly halfway across the world in First Class for the first time in my entire life, one of the most impacting aspects of the trip was visiting the historical sites of Galilee, the Negev and Jerusalem's Old City.

One of the things I immediately noticed as we toured historic sites in the Old City itself was the sheer numbers of pilgrims from all faiths who had come from all over the world to visit places relevant to their faith. Jews come from all over the world to pray at the Western Wall, to see the mountain where Abraham offered Isaac, visit sites where patriarchs, kings and prophets trod centuries ago and to reconnect with their inheritance. Muslims come to pray at the Dome of the Rock and to behold the actual spot they believe Mohammed ascended into heaven. Christians flock to "The Land" to see the places where Jesus walked, was crucified, buried and rose from the dead.

Regardless of their faith or nationality, pilgrims have traveled for centuries and for thousands of miles to have an encounter of spiritual or national significance that will hopefully impact them deeply. That is what a pilgrimage is all about…a journey that changes us dramatically and profoundly.

Psalm 84:5-7 in the Holy Bible talks about such a journey of significance. In the words of the psalmist:

"Blessed are those whose strength is in you, who have set their hearts on pilgrimage. As they pass through the Valley of Baca, they make it a place of springs; the autumn rains also cover it with pools. They go from strength to strength until each appears before God in Zion." NIV

When you have your heart set on something it means you just have to have it. You think about it, you dream about it, your time is consumed in the pursuit of it. The Bible communicates that we are blessed (or happy) when our strength is in God and we have our hearts set on pilgrimage. I would suggest that in the Theotherapy context, the individual's heart is set on a pilgrimage of emotional healing.

The implication is that they have to pass through the Valley of Baca (weeping) to get there. No pain, no gain. What is the Valley of Weeping other than facing deep emotional pain and struggle and working through it? The promise is, however, that as they pass through this place of struggle and deep emotional pain, they make it a place of springs (oasis). In other words, the end result of facing the emotional pain is coming to a place of refreshing, respite and rejuvenation. It goes on to say that the autumn rains also cover it with pools of blessing. In the process, the individuals on this journey get stronger and stronger until they appear before God in Zion. I would suggest that in the process of dealing with our emotional pain, we see resolution come to us through owning and grieving our losses and by taking one step at a time towards that goal of ultimate healing. As a result, we also find that God has been with us every step of the way in our healing journey. We never are completely finished with the whole process until we appear before God in Zion…in other words, until we shuffle off of this mortal coil.

When I was a kid, I wanted to grow up to be three different things: a policeman, a fireman and an archaeologist. I didn't really think about the fact that it would be a challenge to be all three. They all intrigued me but the one that stood out the most to me was the archaeologist. An archaeologist gets to dig around in the dirt and debris for long buried skeletons and artifacts from the distant past. He gets to bring something hidden to light.

I always loved poring over my dad's _National Geographic_ magazines. I loved to read anything to do with dinosaurs, pre-historic men, extinct animals and lost civilizations. I would watch anything I could on television about archaeology and was fascinated with what these scholar-explorers did for a living. I noticed how they would painstakingly and slowly take a soft brush and begin to gently dust away the dirt and debris of centuries. They didn't get in a hurry. They took as long as was necessary to expose what was hidden and to keep it as intact as possible. Years later, I came to see how this same idea of "excavation" applies to the long-hidden secrets and traumas that have shaped our lives as individuals.

We hope to help you "excavate" some painful memories from the past and bring them to light which will mean you are coming out of denial and beginning to look at what makes you tick. Joining me on this pilgrimage means you are giving God permission to excavate your painful memories, to remove what hinders and to preserve what He has ordained for you from before the beginning of time…only a much more healthy version of it. I believe He will show you what to do with it all and will bring you to a deeper place of emotional healing and peace in the process. Dig it?

Mark West
The Theotherapy Project

**A Special Word of Thanks:** I would like to thank Dr. Mario Rivera Mendez, founder of the Theotherapy model of biblical conflict resolution and Luena Darr, Executive Director of Theotherapy Seminars, Incorporated for demonstrating the Theotherapy principles to me with consistency and love. They have been excellent mentors and I am forever grateful for their involvement in my life. Additionally, I would like to thank Dana West and Dorothy Dresser for their invaluable help in organizing and editing this material.

MODULE #1

WHAT IS THEOTHERAPY?

The term "Theotherapy" comes from two Greek words:

"theos" Gk. *(theh'-os)* - God
"therapeuo" Gk. *(ther-ap-yoo'-o)* – to heal

1. All of us need emotional healing whether we know it or not. Sometimes we experience things in life that give us great pain and we don't know what to do about it. When we experience pain in our physical bodies, we go to the doctor to find out what's wrong and to get treatment. We want to get well and feel better. Likewise our emotions can be damaged and need outside intervention for healing. When we receive deep wounds to the soul we often feel disconnected and fractured. That feeling of disconnection and deep emotional pain can cause us a lot of problems in our relationships. It can also affect the choices we make and how we relate to God. We will continue to have all kinds of problems in life until we deal with it effectively.

2. Psychology is the study of man's behavior. Psychology has helped identify sickness in man's soul. Sometimes psychological solutions are perfectly in line with Scripture. Many helpful psychological principles are found in the Word of God, such as forgiveness, resolution of guilt; love to replace fear, etc.

3. Theotherapy is a biblically-based ministry that focuses on emotional conflict resolution. The goal of Theotherapy is to bring about the integration of the spirit, soul and body with a concentrated focus on bringing deep healing to the soul.

   "May God himself, the God of peace, sanctify you through and through. May your whole spirit, soul and body be kept blameless at the coming of our Lord Jesus Christ. The one who calls you is faithful, and he will do it." I Thess. 5:23 *NIV*

4. Just as God has created a natural way for the body to heal from physical wounds, He has created a natural way for the mind to heal. We are emotionally wounded every time we are treated with less than perfect love. God has shown us through His word, the Bible, how *He* deals with the

1

emotional pain of being rejected, abandoned and unloved. He asks us to be like Him in how we resolve our own pain. In Theotherapy we call this the grieving process whereby we choose to forgive and then love those who wounded us.

5. God created us to bring glory to His name. As we use the basic tools of Theotherapy: prayer, confession, resolution of anger, forgiveness, and the acceptance and application of agape (unconditional) love; we will begin to reflect more of Jesus Christ, God's Son, which will glorify Him.

6. We learn in Theotherapy that healing is not so much a specific event at a specific time in an individual's life; it is more like an ongoing journey, a continuing pilgrimage toward healing.

    "Blessed are those whose strength is in you, whose hearts are set on pilgrimage. As they pass through the Valley of Baka, they make it a place of springs; the autumn rains also cover it with pools. They go from strength to strength, till each appears before God in Zion." Psalm 84:5-7 NIV

7. In Theotherapy, we begin to learn "Who Am I"? Who is the real me? As we begin to see and accept the real us, the good and the bad, and that we are valuable to God, we will be able to develop healthy interpersonal relationships and learn that it is sin to live independently from God. We will also become more authentic human beings. When you are "authentic", you can own your strengths and weaknesses equally because neither your strengths nor your weaknesses define you as a person nor do they determine your dignity, worth and significance.

8. Healing and freedom will come as the truth is brought forth in an atmosphere of love and safety. It is our goal in Theotherapy to provide this safe and loving place where God can bring this healing. Even though God may use people and techniques, we know that He is the only one who can bring true and lasting healing. That is what the name *Theotherapy* means – *God heals*.

9. When we are whole (or emotionally healed) people, we are able to:

    a. Love and be loved
    b. Give and receive
    c. Forgive and be forgiven
    d. Understand and be understood

10. When we become more emotionally healed or "whole" our spirit will govern our soul and our body. As we allow the Spirit of God to come into our lives and transform us, He will change all the things that we cannot change about ourselves. As we seek Him for our healing, He will touch the painful places in our lives and restore all that the enemy has stolen.

11. In the process of healing:

    a. The Lord touches our spirit.
    b. Our Spirit touches our soul.
    c. Our Soul touches our body.
    d. And our Body touches others.

12. In the Theotherapy context, we refer to ourselves as "persons in need" (PINs) instead of clients or counselees. We will always be PINs; however, it is our desire in Theotherapy to see God bring us to a place where we can begin to give and receive love more freely (love for God, our neighbor, and ourselves). As we love and are loved, we will be able to exalt and serve God joyfully. The more healing we receive, the more we are able to allow God to be central in all areas and in all aspects of life, instead of trying to live independently from Him.

13. Theotherapy is a biblical method of conflict resolution that draws from many sources:

    a. The Holy Bible
    b. Psychological principles as they are represented in God's Word.
    c. Christian counseling and ministry techniques proven to be effective in emotional healing.

14. In Theotherapy, we believe that all truth ultimately comes from God and must be biblical. Jesus said that the truth will set us free. That is why it is essential to have knowledge of the Bible, the Word of God, as well as a personal relationship with Jesus Christ.

Large Group Dynamic

Unfolding of the rose. Choose a partner. One of you gets to be "the rose" and the other person gets to represent God's unconditional love. The person playing the rose sits in a chair with arms folded, feet crossed, head down and eyes closed. You can even ball up your fists if you want. The person representing God's unconditional love gently starts to release "the rose" into a more relaxed and open position by carefully lifting their chin, asking them to open their eyes, helping them uncross their arms and then to uncross their feet. After the rose is relaxed and open...then switch places. Once you have both experienced being the rose, share how you felt during this dynamic.

*****READ BEFORE STARTING*****

In order for you to complete the Theotherapy program all Study Questions and the Life Applications Sections must be completed and graded. Facilitators may grade Study Questions. The Life Application section will be reviewed by the group leader ONLY. Please don't hesitate to ask for help if needed!!!

Study Questions

1. Complete this sentence; we are emotionally wounded every time we are treated with...
2. In Theotherapy, what do we call dealing with the emotional pain of being rejected, abandoned, and unloved?
3. What does the name Theotherapy mean?
4. List four things we are able to do when we are emotionally healed people.
5. Describe what happens in the process of healing.
6. What do we refer ourselves to in the Theotherapy context?
7. List three sources Theotherapy draws from.
8. In Theotherapy, where do we believe all truth ultimately comes from?

Life Application

1. Write Psalm 84:5-7.
2. What does Psalm 84:5-7 mean to you?
3. Write down one situation that you can remember where you were rejected, abandoned or unloved.
4. Write at least one paragraph about yourself that answers the question: Who am I? Be careful not to tell us about your family, your faith, or your history.
5. Journaling is writing down your thoughts and feelings. It is used by God to work through issues and bring clarity of thought. Before our next session, take some time to write your thoughts and feelings, and even your prayers. Start to listen and see if you hear God talking to you.

MODULE # 2

SEVEN BASIC PRINCIPLES OF THEOTHERAPY

1. We are complex people composed of spirit, soul and body.

a. We are created in the image of God (Genesis 1). God is triune; He has three parts to His being – Father, Son and Holy Spirit. He is perfectly balanced in who He is. We were created to be like Him, so we also have three parts – spirit, soul and body.

b. Our **spirit** is either dead or alive. God makes us alive in Him when we ask for His salvation and choose to be in relationship with Him. Once we are made alive in Jesus Christ our spirit can communicate with God and can know Him intimately.

"But because of his great love for us, God, who is rich in mercy, made us alive with Christ even when we were dead in transgressions—it is by grace you have been saved." Eph. 2:4-5

"Blessed is the one whose transgressions are forgiven, whose sins are covered. Blessed is the one whose sin the Lord does not count against them and in whose spirit is no deceit. For day and night your hand was heavy on me; my strength was sapped as in the heat of summer. Then I acknowledged my sin to you and did not cover up my iniquity. I said, "I will confess my transgressions to the Lord."And you forgave the guilt of my sin. Therefore let all the faithful pray to you while you may be found; surely the rising of the mighty waters will not reach them. You are my hiding place; you will protect me from trouble and surround me with songs of deliverance. I will instruct you and teach you in the way you should go; I will counsel you with my loving eye on you. Do not be like the horse or the mule, which have no understanding but must be controlled by bit and bridle or they will not come to you. Many are the woes of the wicked, but the Lord's unfailing love surrounds the one who trusts in Him. Rejoice in the Lord and be glad, you righteous; sing, all you who are upright in heart!" Psalm 32 NIV

c. Our **soul** reflects our personality. It is the part of us that contains our conflicts and beliefs and is made up of our intellect (thinker), our emotions (feeler) and our will (chooser). We are in need of daily cleansing and healing in each of these areas.

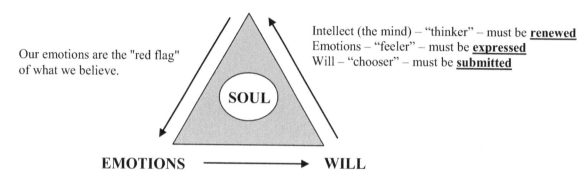

INTELLECT - Where the lie is rooted

Intellect (the mind) – "thinker" – must be **renewed**
Emotions – "feeler" – must be **expressed**
Will – "chooser" – must be **submitted**

Our emotions are the "red flag" of what we believe.

SOUL

EMOTIONS ⟶ **WILL**

THE GRIEVING PROCESS
*SHOCK
*ANGER
*SADNESS
*BARGAINING
*RESOLUTION = FORGIVENESS
(an act of the will)

With our will we choose to believe the "truth that sets us free"…. Choosing to believe the truth destroys the lies in our belief systems that hinder us.

> *Important note: The stages of grief are outlined in greater detail in Module 11 (Grief) pages 64-68. This will help you understand what the grieving process looks like.*

1) Our mind must be **renewed**.

> *"Do not conform any longer to the pattern of this world, but be transformed by the renewing of your mind. Then you will be able to test and approve what God's will is – His good, pleasing, and perfect will." Romans 12:2 NIV*

2) Our feelings must be **expressed** in a manner that will bring healing and not more conflict. We must never "vent" on another person, but at the same time we need to learn to honestly express our feelings and resolve them in healthy ways.

> *"In your anger do not sin. Do not let the sun go down while you are still angry, and do not give the devil a foothold." Ephesians 4:26 NIV*

> *"Blessed are they who mourn, for they will be comforted." Matthew 5:4 NIV*

3) Our will needs to be completely **submitted** to God. He never takes away our freedom of choice, but he wants us to realize that His way is always best because He always has our best interest at heart. We get to choose, however, whether or not we will submit our will to His healing.

> *"When the pain of staying the same becomes greater than the pain of changing...we change!"* Dr. Mario Rivera

> *"Then Jesus said to His disciples, "If anyone would come after me, he must deny himself, and take up his cross and follow me."* Matthew 16:24 NIV

d. Our **body** is the part of us that is in contact with the rest of the world. It is the temple/dwelling place for our spirit and soul. The Bible calls it our *"jar of clay"*...I sometimes refer to it as my *"earth suit"*. God wants each of us to take care of our body and not abuse it, because it is through our body that our spirit and soul find expression.

2. All of us have dignity, worth and significance as God's creation (*Genesis 1, 2*).

We also have depravity as a result of our rebellion against God our Creator (Genesis 3). We need to repent from living independently from God, being led by His love to turn away from our rebellion against Him. As we allow the Lord to deal with our depravity...our dignity, worth and significance will return.

1) *dignity* – dig-ni-ty – the state or quality of being worthy of honor or respect.

2) *worth* – sufficiently good, important, or interesting to justify a specified action; deserving to be treated or regarded in the way specified.

3) *significance* - sig-nif-i-cance – the quality of being worthy of attention; importance.

4) *depravity* - de-prav-i-ty – the innate corruptness of human nature, due to original sin.

3. There is no healing without a true expression of feeling.

This is God's natural way of healing our emotions. Confessing the truth and feeling the pain connected to the buried fear, guilt, anger and unforgiveness in our hearts is the first step. Releasing our feelings helps us to begin the grieving process that is absolutely necessary for the resolution of losses. After resolving our losses, we will then be able to embrace the faith, hope and love that God has for us. With our will we choose to believe the "truth that sets us free".... Choosing to believe the truth destroys the lies in our belief systems that hinder us.

4. Good THEOLOGY is good PSYCHOLOGY.

a. An accurate understanding of the unconditional love of God we have in Jesus Christ is the basis of sound mental health. Misunderstanding or ignoring God and His purposes can lead to all types of mental and emotional problems.

b. Throughout our life we develop our own belief systems, many of which have their origin in lies that we have come to believe. Once these lies are discovered, they can be replaced with the truth of God's Word, bringing healing to the deep wounds of the soul.

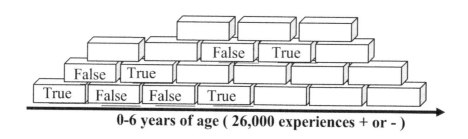

0-6 years of age (26,000 experiences + or -)

c. Each of these experiences creates either a true or false building block in our "belief system". Those building blocks are the foundation of what we believe about ourselves and what we believe about God's character. Our true building blocks are the true things we believe about God and ourselves. The false building blocks come as a result of negative feelings we transfer to God based on our experiences as a child.

d. We will tend to "transfer" to God the way we viewed our parents in our family of origin. For example: *"My parents were always angry or distant...therefore, God must be angry and distant."* Or, *"My parents gave me money or things to show their love rather than just being with me…therefore, if God doesn't give me the "things" I ask for…He must not really love me."*

5. **We do not have problems, we are the problem.**

   We cannot go on blaming people or situations in our past or present for our problems. Even if a person purposely sinned against us, we are responsible for our own actions and reactions to what has happened to us. No one can make us feel a certain way; *we choose to feel how we feel.* How we see things, and our responses, are our problems, and only we can change these things. We cannot change the other person, only God can. As we begin to see things through God's perspective, we are set free from victimization, powerlessness, and the need for revenge. It is God's will to help us to diffuse the past, conquer the present, and have hope for the future. No one can accomplish this for us; however, our relationship with God in Jesus Christ gives us all the resources we need to bring about positive and lasting change.

6. **When we have effectively dealt with the past, we will be able to effectively deal with the present**.

   The **Negative Active Past (NAP)** is the result of unresolved conflicts and unmet needs from our past that continue to invade our present. Our present day relationships become a dumping ground for the buried anger, fear and guilt that we have never dealt with. We keep demanding people in our present to pay for the pain others from our past have caused us. By carefully observing our actions and reactions in our present circumstances, we can learn to touch the feelings we never expressed from the past and resolve them.

7. **Once we have faced the unmet needs in our lives, and have begun to let them go by grieving, God will step in and fill those needs.** Our parents were chosen by God to be the vessels for our creation. They were entrusted with our early training and were meant to teach us about God as our source and hope of salvation. Because our parents could not meet the deepest needs in our hearts that can only be truly met by God alone, we suffer a loss as we grow up. We were created for unconditional love, but we are doomed to receive the imperfect love of our broken and sinful parents. When we face the fact that our parents cannot be everything to us, we are set free to grieve the loss of unconditional love in our lives and how that affected us. We are free to look to God to fulfill our needs as He sees fit instead of always searching for some person or thing to meet our deepest needs. Letting go of the control we have allowed others to have in our lives is how we are able to gain the life that Jesus Christ has for us.

JUST FYI

Excavating Two Types of Wounds...

There are two types of wounds: type A and type B. Both types can be equally devastating.

Type A – When we never received something we needed (unconditional love, acceptance, attention, time, nurture, etc.) With type A wounds we can comprehend a vacuum or a "lack of" something significant in our lives, particularly in our family of origin.

Type B – When someone does something directly to us that traumatizes us deeply (physical, sexual, emotional abuse, shaming or embarrassing us, overt rejection and abandonment).

*****READ BEFORE STARTING*****

In order for you to complete the Theotherapy program all Study Questions and the Life Applications Sections must be completed and graded. Facilitators may grade Study Questions. The Life Application section will be reviewed by the group leader ONLY. Please don't hesitate to ask for help if needed!!!

Study Questions

1. List the seven basic principles of Theotherapy.
2. List the three parts of our being.
3. What happens to our spirit when we accept Jesus Christ as our savior and Lord according to Eph. 2:4-5?
4. What part of our being contains our conflicts and beliefs?
5. What part of our being needs to be renewed?
6. What part of our being needs to be completely submitted to God?

Life Application

1. Describe your relationship with Jesus Christ
.

2. If you do not have a relationship with Jesus Christ, we invite you to begin a relationship with Him through making the following prayer your personal prayer.

   Father, I confess that I am a sinner and that there is no salvation except through Jesus Christ. I repent of my independence from you and trying to live my life apart from you. Please forgive me Father for all of my sins, and create in me a clean heart. I invite you into all of my life to transform me and make me a new creature in Christ Jesus. I believe that Jesus Christ is the Son of the living God, that He died for my sins, and that He arose from the dead into eternal life. I invite His Holy Spirit to come and dwell within me, in the name of Jesus Christ, Amen.

   "If you confess with your mouth, 'Jesus is Lord,' and believe in your heart that God raised Him from the dead, you will be saved."
   Romans 10:9

   Welcome to the family of God! You are now an heir to God's Kingdom, with His gift of eternal life. Your spirit has been changed from death to life. God says all of those who come to Him, He will in no way cast out but will make them co-heirs with Christ Jesus. You can now come boldly to God's throne of grace and find help in your time of need. Congratulations!

   Briefly describe what this means to you and if you have prayed this prayer, be sure to tell someone.

3. In the FYI section of this module two different types of wounds are described. What are they?

4. Write a "Who Am I" paper describing yourself without telling us what you do or who your family is, or where you grew up.

MODULE # 3

THE NEGATIVE ACTIVE PAST (NAP)

1. The Negative Active Past (NAP) is a phrase we use in Theotherapy to describe how unresolved events from the past affect our present day circumstances. When we suffer pain, loss, or any negative emotion, that emotion stays inside until it is dealt with by **grieving** and **forgiving**.

2. Until the NAP is resolved, past events will be expressed in reactions that are out of proportion to what the current situation warrants. These intense feelings and reactions are indicators of the fact that the negative things of the past are still very much alive and at work within us.

   a. In the Theotherapy context, when we over react to a current situation, we refer to that reaction as being "triggered". In other words, the current situation "triggers" a very negative memory from our past. As a result of being triggered, we may have over reacted and as a result of our over-reaction, we now know that we have some deeper work to do in resolving the painful memory.

   b. Feelings are timeless. They do not change, grow old, or just "go away". They need to be "intelligently" expressed with a corresponding change in your belief system.

   c. Our negative emotions are tied in with the lies that we began to believe as a result of the negative experiences we had in our past.

   • Remember the building blocks we talked about in Module Two? Each of our experiences between the ages of zero and six creates either a true or false building block in our belief system. These building blocks are the foundation of what we believe about ourselves as well as what we believe about God's character. Our true building blocks are the true things we believe about God and ourselves. The false building blocks come as a result of lies we begin to believe about ourselves, about God, love, sin, the Church, the Bible etc., because of the negative things that happened to us.

d. Until we successfully deal with our pain, grief, and losses, we will not be able to change and grow into the emotionally whole person that God has *called* us to be.

"For those God foreknew, He also predestined to be conformed to the likeness of His Son, that He might be the firstborn among many brothers." Romans 8:29 NIV

3. Diffusion (De-Activation) of the NAP.

   a. It is very important for us to "process through" the conflict and allow GOD to clean up those painful areas and show us the lies we began to believe as a result of the conflict. The lies must then be replaced with the truth that sets us free.

   b. This is what it looks like to go through the Valley of Baca (weeping) Psalm 84:5-7. No pain, no gain.

   c. We must admit our present feelings. We must "own" what has happened and recognize what it has cost us and those we care about.

      1) We need to face the truth of what has happened to us in the past and come out of denial.

      Jesus said, "Then you will know the truth and the truth will set you free."
      John 8:32 NIV

      2) Link past hurts to our present feelings and current circumstances. We should then ask God to show us what past event is connected with the feelings we are now experiencing.

      3) We must express our feelings to the depth and significance of the initial source of pain. This is critical in the healing process because if we don't really look at the source of the pain, we will just skim the surface and not really deal with it completely.

      4) We must allow ourselves to express our feelings in a safe environment that does not produce more pain. (for example: journaling or role play.)

      5) Use the forgiveness letter model (see page 15 for forgiveness letter).

6) In a role play, you get with someone you trust and have them pretend to be the person who hurt you. (You get to tell them exactly how you feel about what they did and how it has affected you).

7) Ask God to show you what lie you have believed as a result of the event you are dealing with.

8) Forgive or cancel the debt of the one who sinned against you.

   a) Let go of the things you believe others owe you and recognize that only Jesus has what you need.

   b) Let go of expecting people in your present to pay for what others in your past have done to you!

9) Recognize that you are responsible for letting God change you and choosing to believe the truth instead of the lie. (You don't have problems, you are the problem!).

In summary, the following steps are needed in order to diffuse the Negative Active Past.

- Admit our present feelings.
- Link past hurts to our present feelings.
- Express our feelings to the depth and significance of the initial source of pain.
- Discover the lie we have believed as a result of the painful experience.
- Forgive/cancel the debt
- Recognize that you are responsible for letting God change you and choosing to believe the truth instead of the lie.

We have included the following outline to assist you in Diffusing the NAP. It is in the form of a letter but you don't actually send it. We will discuss forgiveness more in Module #6.

Dear _____,
I remember when *(write down what happened to you)*...

As a result of what I experienced, I felt *(make sure to allow yourself to feel the feelings that you list here)*....

I began to think or believe *(what lies did you believe about yourself as a result of what you experienced?)* ....

The consequences of what I experienced were *(what did the event or trauma cost you in your life? How has it affected your life, relationships and decisions?)*...

Today I am making a decision to forgive you through the death and blood of Jesus Christ just as **HE** has forgiven me. With this I am letting go of...(list what you are letting go of...for example: *bitterness, resentment, hatred, etc.)* and am asking God to heal the wounds and lies I have believed as a result. I now ask God to give me His unconditional love for _____.

JUST FYI

More Theo-therapeutic Tools....
Another useful tool we utilize in Theotherapy is the use of **imagination** on the part of the PIN. Sometimes we will ask a person to imagine Jesus coming into a place of pain in their childhood. We understand that time; space or historical events do not limit God. He, being omniscient, omnipotent and omnipresent was there when they were wounded or abused though He was not physically seen.

When a child is traumatized and rejected, they often believe they were unloved and alone. Believing this keeps them trapped in the fear and rejection they experienced in the trauma. Asking the PIN to imagine Jesus coming into that scenario often helps to diffuse the lies they have believed and also helps them realize Jesus was present, aware of their pain and loving them through it (I John 4:18; John 8:32).

In order for you to complete the Theotherapy program all Study Questions and the Life Applications Sections must be completed and graded. Facilitators may grade Study Questions. The Life Application section will be reviewed by the group leader ONLY. Please don't hesitate to ask for help if needed!!!

Study Questions
1. What does the term "Negative Active Past" mean?
2. How are negative emotions effectively dealt with?
3. What do we mean by "feelings are timeless"?
4. List the six steps needed to diffuse the Negative Active Past.

Life Application
1. Ask the Lord to speak to you as you answer the following questions and thank Him for His presence. He is with you right now!
2. What feelings are you struggling with in your life at this time?
3. How are these feelings connected to something that happened in your past? Here are some phrases that may help you with this.

    a. _____reminds me of my mother/father
    because_____.
    b. I get "triggered" when
    _____.
    c. A particular sound, smell, song or color brings me to the memory of
    _____.
    d. The room in my childhood home I remember most is
    _____.

4. Either write out or verbally go through the forgiveness letter addressing the person involved in the earlier event that is linked to your present feelings if possible.
5. Write down and/or express your feelings as much as you possibly can.
6. If you chose to write a forgiveness letter, you may wish to destroy it when you are finished.

7. Ask God to give you His love and His forgiveness for the person to whom you wrote your forgiveness letter.
8. Cancel that person's debt to you.
9. Briefly tell us what this experience meant to you.

MODULE # 4

ANGER

1. God is our model for justifiable anger.

- God became angry when He was **rejected** - *"...they provoked the Lord to anger because they forsook Him and served Baal and Ashtoreths." Judges 2:12&13.*
- God became angry when He was **abandoned** by His people - *"Yet my people have forgotten me..." Jeremiah 18:15a.*
- God became angry when He was **used** - *"...They have turned their backs to me and not their faces; yet when they are in trouble, they say, 'Come and save us!'" Jeremiah 2:27.*
- God became angry when He was **criticized** - *"How long will this wicked community grumble against me?" Numbers 14:27.*
- God became angry when He was **not wanted** - *"...they have perverted their ways and have forgotten the Lord their God." Jeremiah 3:21.*

JUST FYI

Repressed Anger...

People repress their anger because they think angry feelings are sinful. When a person's anger surfaces in Theotherapy, we may encourage them to express their anger verbally and/or physically by using a sock bat or by stomping their feet. After a person has released these negative emotions in a way that does not harm themselves or others, they will have a greater sense of emotional freedom. Jesus expressed His anger in a physical manner when God's temple had been misused by the moneychangers (John 2:12-17). Anger is not good or bad in and of itself...it is what we do with it that determines whether or not it is healthy.

2. We also have justifiable anger.

    a. God designed us to be loved unconditionally. When we are rejected, abandoned, used, scorned, or criticized, there is a loss and it produces pain. This emotional pain causes anger. It is the natural and God-given response to pain and loss. We are created in His image so the same things that make God angry make us angry.

    b. Even when our anger is justifiable, if we choose to hold on to it, it produces bitterness, malice, desire for revenge, etc. Consequently, we are really just hurting ourselves.

"Be angry, but sin not..." Ephesians 4:26 KJV

3. What is sinful anger?

    a. Anger becomes sinful when we allow the sun to go down and make no effort to resolve it. When we "go to sleep on it," we often suppress some of the emotion attached to it and therefore don't fully resolve it. If we don't resolve it, we move it to a deeper level of bitterness, malice, and the desire for revenge. Later on, when a similar event happens, the unresolved anger will surface again when we are triggered by a person or event. Often the resulting reaction will be way out of proportion to what the current situation actually warrants because we have "stuffed" the anger and have made no real effort to resolve it.

"...Do not let the sun go down while you are still angry, and donot give the devil a foothold (stronghold)." Ephesians 4:26 NIV

       • A stronghold is a place of bondage to a particular sin or thought pattern. The enemy (Satan) uses the wounds in our lives to establish strongholds of pain, depression, feelings of failure, sinful behaviors, and fear. Deliverance is the action of being rescued or set free.

"Demons dwell in the structures of unforgiveness." Francis Frangipane

    b. Another example of sinful anger is when we take out our anger on others or on ourselves in ways that bring about physical or emotional harm.

c. When we are in denial and don't want to face it, we will tend to internalize our anger. Unresolved anger turned inward can cause serious depression. This is very unhealthy and can result in actually causing physical symptoms (psychosomatic illnesses).

- *psychosomatic* – psy-cho-so-mat-ic – a physical illness or other condition caused or aggravated by a mental factor such as unresolved internal conflict or stress.

d. Our anger is sinful when we have inappropriate transference. If we look to others in our present to try to make them pay for the pain caused by people in our past, it only produces disappointment, frustration and more anger. People in our present will never be able to meet our unfulfilled needs or expectations.

4. Resolution

a. Own your anger (be totally honest about it).

b. Express the anger in a way that doesn't hurt anyone. There are many things we can do to validate our anger and express it in healthy ways rather than destructive ways. Some healthy ways to express anger are:

1) Hit your bed or a chair with a sock bat or scream into a pillow.

2) Exercise, jog, or hit a punching bag *while you process* through your angry thoughts.

3) Journal or write a letter to the person you are angry with (but don't mail it)!

4) Tell God all about it. He knows how you feel and can handle it.

5) Do a role-play with someone you trust.

c. Apply God's true model of forgiveness from the heart:

1) We have to acknowledge what has happened to us, and accept the fact that we are **POWERLESS** to change it.

20

2) We must surrender all desire for revenge or retaliation. We must surrender the right to get even. We have to let go of trying to control the situation and allow God to change the other person.

3) We must experience enough true emotional healing to have the freedom to be able to say from the heart:

"It doesn't matter if you reject me. You don't have the power to hurt me."

d. Appropriate Transference

1) At the cross, God transferred His anger onto Jesus.

2) God transfers our guilt and shame onto Jesus.

3) Then God transfers Christ's righteousness on to us. This is called the *justification* process.

*****READ BEFORE STARTING*****

In order for you to complete the Theotherapy program all Study Questions and the Life Applications Sections must be completed and graded. Facilitators may grade Study Questions. The Life Application section will be reviewed by the group leader ONLY. Please don't hesitate to ask for help if needed!!!

Study Questions
1. List all five examples of when God gets angry.
2. Give four examples of sinful anger.
3. List four steps to resolution of anger.

Life Application
1. Can you see areas in your life where you are still angry?
2. Are you angry at yourself for anything?
3. Who are you most angry with today?

4. Take this time to go through the four steps to resolution of anger with this person now using the tools available to you.
5. Do you believe that you have come to a place of resolution in this situation?
6. Why?

MODULE # 5

REJECTION

"Rejection is a root planted when we are young. It becomes how we perceive the world."
Ed Odom

1. Man experienced his first rejection in the Garden of Eden

    a. When man sinned, it separated him from God. As a result of his sin, man felt this separation and because of his disobedience could no longer remain in the Garden of Eden. Man thought that God had rejected him. God did not reject man…man rejected God. God used this feeling of rejection for the *purpose of putting in man's heart a thirst for God.* (Genesis 3)

    b. God, in His mercy, takes our feelings of rejection and uses them to create in us a desire for relationship with God.

    > *"As the deer pants for streams of water, so my soul pants for you, my God. My soul thirsts for God, for the living God. When can I go and meet with God?" Psalm 42:1-2 NIV*

2. We all have been rejected, even Jesus.

    a. Jesus became human so He could identify with us. He wanted to feel what we feel and to experience all of the things that cause us pain. He wanted us to know that God cares deeply about everything we go through in life. He came because He loved us…yet…

    > *"He was despised and rejected by men, a man of sorrows, and familiar with suffering. Like one from whom men hide their faces He was despised, and we esteemed Him not." Isaiah 53:3 NIV*

    b. We feel rejected when we need love and there is no one to give it or when we give love and there is no one to receive it. The need for unconditional love is as critical as our need for food and water.

    c. Rejection is a psychological feeling. Sometimes we feel rejected because we expect it or we think we somehow deserve it. We get the first feelings of rejection from our parents, whether they intended to hurt us or not. We tend to think God is like our parents. If my parents rejected me…then I expect God to reject me.

23

d. All "embraced" rejection is self rejection. If we know that we are loved, no one can effectively reject us; however, if we feel unloved, we form barriers to protect ourselves. We then blame others for hurting and rejecting us; but in reality, we are rejecting ourselves.

3. Any time we experience rejection, it can be harmful and very painful.

   a. The first six years of our lives are especially important in our development as human beings. It is during the first six years that our core belief about who we are, who God is, and our belief about our place in this world is established.

   b. Parents communicate acceptance in a variety of ways: teaching, spending time with their children, listening, disciplining, and by showing affection.

   c. Because children get their value by how their parents treat them, when children are ignored, they feel worthless.

   "Can a mother forget the baby at her breast and have no compassion on the child she has borne? Though she may forget, I will not forget you! See, I have engraved you on the palms of my hands; your walls are ever before me." Isaiah 49:15-16 NIV

4. What is the cure for rejection?

   a. Rejection must be brought into the light. In order to do this, we must see and accept the truth about why we feel rejected. As we discover and touch the truth of what happened, even when it hurts, rejection will begin to lose its power over us.

   "But if we walk in the light, as He is in the light, we have fellowship with one another, and the blood of Jesus, His Son, purifies us from all sin." I John 1:7 NIV

   b. As we address our pent up emotions by feeling the pain and releasing it, usually by crying significantly, we will break rejection's power over us. This is called having a catharsis. There must also be a corresponding change in our belief system in order to finally be free from the pain.

   - *catharsis* – ca-thar-sis - the process of releasing, and thereby providing relief from, strong or repressed emotions.

"Jesus wept." John 11:35 NIV

"As He (Jesus) approached Jerusalem and saw the city, He wept over it..."
Luke 19:41 NIV

"Blessed are you who weep now, for you will laugh." Luke 6:21 NIV

c. Confessing our sins removes the separation that sin brings. Confession brings us out of denial and allows us to heal and also helps heal our relationships.

> *"Therefore confess your sins to each other and pray for each other so that you may be healed." James 5:16b NIV*

1) I must accept God's forgiveness, before I can truly and deeply forgive others. After all, you can't give away something you don't have yourself.

2) Self rejection is actually a sin. As an act of our will, the Lord wants us to receive His love for us, even if we don't feel it. He wants us to walk by faith in what He says. He says that NOTHING can separate us from His love.

> *"For I am convinced that neither death nor life, neither angels nor demons, neither the present, nor the future, nor any powers, neither height nor depth, nor anything else in all of creation, will be able to separate us from the love of God that is in Christ Jesus our Lord." Romans 8:38-39 NIV*

3) I must truly and deeply forgive the one who hurt me. When I do this, I no longer expect that person to pay for the painful way they treated me.

> *"If I don't forgive, it's like I am choosing to drink a glass of deadly poison and expecting the other person to drop dead. The person who hurt me may not even remember how they hurt me, yet I may be holding on to them expecting them to somehow change or fix the situation. That gives them power over me." Anonymous*

4) I must experience God's unconditional love in order to heal from the pain of rejection. (Gal. 5:22). Unconditional love (agape) is the perfect antidote for rejection.

> *"But the fruit of the Spirit is love, joy peace, patience, kindness, goodness, faithfulness, gentleness and self-control. Against such things there is no law."* Galatians 5:22 NIV

d. Forgiveness is not an emotion. It is a decision of the will.

- Make up your mind that you are going to forgive and God will take you through the process of truly forgiving others and even yourself. This puts us in proper relationship with God.

> *"But I tell you: Love your enemies and pray for those who persecute you, that you may be sons of your Father in heaven."* Matthew 5:44

JUST FYI

Excavating the Child within...

A person who has experienced rejection and abandonment in childhood tends to abandon him or herself. They often feel guilty for even existing. They ignore the pain of rejection and abandonment or try to "numb" it with some sort of emotional narcotic (food, shopping, sex, work, obsession with church activities, etc.) In Theotherapy we help persons connect to the little child within them and we minister to that inner child so that the person can mature and take hold of all God has for them without having to run to other things to numb the pain. *"But Jesus said, 'Let the children come to me, and do not hinder them, for the kingdom of God belongs to such as these...'"* Luke 18:16

Large Group Dynamic

Rejection Circle – Caution: Use this dynamic carefully. While your group is sitting, have them number off: "one," "two", "one," "two"…until every person in the group is either a one or a two. Have all the "ones" form a circle and face outward. Have all the number "twos" form a circle around the number ones while facing them. All the people in the inner circle will stand still and watch the faces and body language of the outer circle as it rotates around the inner circle.

The outer circle will say nothing, but will communicate rejection with their facial expressions and body language. Encourage all participants in this dynamic to allow themselves to feel the pain of their own rejection. Let the outside circle rotate slowly around the inside circle several times. Then have them return to their seats and write down their thoughts and feelings about any memories of rejection that were brought to the surface in this dynamic. Then ask some really brave ones to share what they have written, felt or remembered.

*****READ BEFORE STARTING*****

In order for you to complete the Theotherapy program all Study Questions and the Life Applications Sections must be completed and graded. Facilitators may grade Study Questions. The Life Application section will be reviewed by the group leader ONLY. Please don't hesitate to ask for help if needed!!!

Study Questions
1. When and where did man experience his first feeling of rejection?
2. Why did God allow this to happen?
3. What does it mean that God wants us to thirst after Him?
4. What is rejection?
5. Explain the statement "all embraced rejection is self-rejection.

Life Application
1. Rejection is always harmful. Write or think about one especially harmful experience of rejection you remember most vividly from childhood.

2. Use the grieving and forgiveness steps you have learned so far to bring about resolution to this painful memory. Let us know if you need some help. Remember the Holy Spirit is the wonderful counselor and He is always with you.

3. Share with us how this has helped you.

MODULE # 6

FORGIVENESS

"Therefore, the kingdom of heaven is like a king who wanted to settle accounts with his servants. As he began the settlement, a man who owed him ten thousand bags of gold was brought to him. Since he was not able to pay, the master ordered that he and his wife and his children and all that he had be sold to repay the debt. At this the servant fell on his knees before him. 'Be patient with me,' he begged, 'and I will pay back everything.' The servant's master took pity on him, canceled the debt and let him go. But when that servant went out, he found one of his fellow servants who owed him a hundred silver coins. He grabbed him and began to choke him. 'Pay back what you owe me!' he demanded. His fellow servant fell to his knees and begged him, 'Be patient with me, and I will pay it back.' But he refused. Instead, he went off and had the man thrown into prison until he could pay the debt. When the other servants saw what had happened, they were outraged and went and told their master everything that had happened. Then the master called the servant in. 'You wicked servant,' he said, 'I canceled all that debt of yours because you begged me to. Shouldn't you have had mercy on your fellow servant just as I had on you?' In anger his master handed him over to the jailers to be tortured, until he should pay back all he owed. This is how my heavenly Father will treat each of you unless you forgive your brother or sister from your heart." Matthew 18:23-35 NIV

1. What is forgiveness?

   a. We were created to be loved perfectly. Unfortunately, even in the best situations we are never going to be properly loved all the time. This leaves us all in a place of need. From our birth, every relationship will be less than perfect. We cannot meet the other person's need for love, and our need for love cannot be fully met by them. We all have debts to pay and debts others owe us. The way that we deal with our IOU's is to give and receive forgiveness.

   b. Definition: forgiveness is releasing the one whom we feel is indebted to us. We give all of our **IOU's** to the Lord. When we forgive, we release the offender from the expectation that they should somehow make it right with us or that they should have to submit to our desire for retribution, retaliation or revenge. We cannot, however, do anything about the law of sowing and reaping they will experience as a result of their choices. That part is up to God. We give up the resentment and anger toward the offender as well as the desire for vengeance.

c. Forgiveness is commanded by the Lord

"And be ye kind one to another, tenderhearted, forgiving one another, even as God for Christ's sake hath forgiven you." Ephesians 4:32 NIV

d. Forgiveness is an act of our will, not an emotion.

- We reap what we have sown. The law of sowing and reaping is a universal law God established during creation. It is what it is and nothing can change that law other than by God's divine intervention.

"If you do not forgive men their sins, your Father will not forgive your sins." Matthew 6:15 NIV

e. The root of unforgiveness is unresolved anger.

f. Types of forgiveness:

1) Forgiveness we receive for salvation.

a) We must see ourselves as sinners but not as failures.

"For all have sinned, and come short of the glory of God." Romans 3:23

b) We are born into sin with the need to forgive and be forgiven.

"All we like sheep have gone astray; we have turned every one to his own way; and the Lord hath laid on Him the iniquity of us all." Isaiah 53:6 NIV

2) Forgiveness for daily sins.

"If we confess our sins, He is faithful and just to forgive us our sins, and to cleanse us from all unrighteousness." I John 1:9 NIV

3) Forgiveness we extend to others.

"And when ye stand praying, forgive, if ye have aught against any; that your Father also which is in heaven may forgive you your trespasses." Mark 11:25KJV

4) Forgiveness others extend to us.

> *"Forgiveness is not an occasional act...it is a permanent attitude."*
> Dr. Martin Luther King, Jr.

> *"I will not permit any man to narrow and degrade my soul by making me hate him."*
> Booker T. Washington

2. How to Forgive

   a. We can only forgive to the degree that we have received forgiveness.

      1) We must receive forgiveness from God.

      2) We must extend forgiveness to others.

      3) We must forgive ourselves.

      Jesus replied: "'Love the Lord your God with all your heart and with all your soul and with all your mind' This is the first and greatest commandment. And the second is like it: 'Love your neighbor as yourself.' Matthew 22:37-39 NIV

   b. We can only forgive to the degree that we feel the pain of the offense.

      1) Time itself does not heal wounds caused by sin.

         " I, the LORD your God, am a jealous God, punishing the children for the sin of the parents to the third and fourth generation of those who hate me." Exodus 20:5b NIV

      2) Real Forgiveness comes from our heart, not from our head.

         In anger his master handed him over to the jailers to be tortured, until he should pay back all he owed. "This is how my heavenly Father will treat each of you unless you forgive your brother or sister from your heart." Matthew 18:34-35 NIV

c. We must take responsibility for our sins.

   1) No matter how much we have been hurt and sinned against, if we don't forgive the offender, we are sinning ourselves.

   "Even if they sin against you seven times in a day and seven times come back to you saying 'I repent,' you must forgive them." Luke 17:4 NIV

   2) Many times, we hold unforgiveness against the Lord. While God certainly does not sin and therefore does not need to be forgiven, we often transfer the anger we have against others or even ourselves to God. We sometimes blame God for the bad things that happen to us. God understands our misdirected anger and is willing to help us work through it. Confessing our anger to Him is a way of coming clean and it also opens the door for Him to show us the root of our anger as well as the truth that will set us free.

d. We will have a need for receiving and giving forgiveness until the day we die.

*****READ BEFORE STARTING*****

In order for you to complete the Theotherapy program all Study Questions and the Life Applications Sections must be completed and graded. Facilitators may grade Study Questions. The Life Application section will be reviewed by the group leader ONLY. Please don't hesitate to ask for help if needed!!!

Study Questions
   1. How do we deal with our IOU's?
   2. Can you really forgive without touching the pain of the offense?
   3. What is the root of unforgiveness?
   4. List the four types of forgiveness.

Life Application
   1. Can you think of some people that you thought that you forgave but still need to forgive more? Many times the Lord leads us to forgive people we

think we have already forgiven. This is because forgiveness comes in layers. The Lord will not require more of us than we can bear. Can you remember someone who you need to forgive, or forgive at a different level?

2. Write a forgiveness letter to one of them. Do not send the letter. We have listed the things you need to say in your letter below

Dear.....
I remember when ...
As a result I felt.....
I began to think (or believe).....
Today I am making a decision to forgive you through the death and blood of Jesus Christ, just as **HE** has forgiven me. With this I am letting go of........
I am asking God to give me His love for you and to heal the wounds and lies I have believed as a result.

Signed_____
Date_____

3. I now choose to let _____ off the hook.

MODULE # 7

EXISTENTIAL GUILT (real or "normal" guilt)

1. There are two kinds of guilt: existential (healthy) guilt and neurotic (unhealthy) guilt. In this module we will discuss Existential Guilt All of us have experienced feelings of guilt from time to time. Often feelings of guilt are warranted due to our wrong actions or attitudes.

2. Existential guilt is *healthy* guilt, which should exist when we have willfully made bad choices. Existential guilt results when we know we have broken God's commands or have done something wrong: morally, legally, or ethically.

3. Existential guilt is the kind of guilt God uses to get our attention when we have done something wrong to someone else because we were being selfish. Perhaps we went against our better judgment and made a really bad choice that affected us or others in a very negative way. Maybe we said or did something unkind that we can never take back. Existential guilt exists until we diffuse it by confession and repentance.

   "If we confess our sins, he is faithful and just and will forgive us our sins and purify us from all unrighteousness." 1 John 1:9 NIV

   "For all have sinned and fall short of the glory of God." Romans 3:23 NIV

4. With existential guilt, the reason for the guilt is known - it is the result of our choice to sin. We are convicted and we *should* feel guilty. We know that we have sinned, yet we have not done anything about it.

5. Typical guilt development

   a. We choose to sin: When we want to do things our way and not God's way, that's when we fall into Satan's trap. Sin looks and feels so good, because we do not believe that God's way really is best.

34

Imagine you decided to go fishing early one morning. As you walk up to the edge of the lake, you see another fisherman there with a string full of fish. What is the first question you would ask him? Most of us would probably ask him what kind of bait he was using. We would want to know the answer to that important question because we would also want to have a string full of fish at the end of the day.

I know a guy who used to live in the Seattle area and loved to fly fish. He spent a lot of time finding out what the trout or salmon were biting on. He would even make his own "flies" or would find out what the hottest most effective lures were at the moment. He spent a great deal of time perfecting his "cast" and could really make the "fly" look like it was skimming across the water. Sometimes, he caught a lot of fish...other times he didn't fare so well. It all boiled down to what the fish felt like eating that day. No matter how good you are as a fisherman...if the fish aren't interested...you can walk away with nothing more than bad sunburn and a great deal of frustration. You can't make a fish bite. They have to *take the bait.*

Satan cannot make us sin...but he has spent centuries watching what kinds of things cause mankind to "take the bait" and fall into sin. In fact, he knows what things you and I tend to resort to when we are emotionally empty. We want something to make that empty feeling go away. Of course, he loves to make the bait he offers look really good and he is a very skilled "fisherman". He throws out the line with the bait and then he watches to see whether or not we will actually take the bait. Sometimes we do...and sometimes we don't. When we do take the bait, we usually get more than we bargained for in guilt, shame and regrets. Satan makes it all seem so good...but what he offers always brings devastation, destruction and bondage. He can't make us take the bait...but he sure can hook us and get us on his string if we do decide to take it.

"Choosing rather to suffer affliction with the people of God, than to enjoy the pleasures of sin for a season;" Hebrews 11:25 KJV

b. Once we have taken the bait and have been hooked, we are accused by Satan: He cheers us on to commit sin, and then he becomes our persecutor, and our greatest accuser.

> *"Then the LORD said to Satan, 'Have you considered my servant Job? There is no one on earth like him; he is blameless and upright, a man who fears God and shuns evil.' "Does Job fear God for nothing?" Satan replied. "Have you not put a hedge around him and his household and everything he has? You have blessed the work of his hands, so that his flocks and herds are spread throughout the land. But now stretch out your hand and strike everything he has, and he will surely curse you to your face." Job 1:8-11 NIV*

> *"Jesus, full of the Holy Spirit, left the Jordan and was led by the Spirit into the wilderness, where for forty days he was tempted by the devil. He ate nothing during those days, and at the end of them he was hungry. The devil said to him, "If you are the Son of God, tell this stone to become bread." Jesus answered, "It is written: 'Man shall not live on bread alone.'" The devil led him up to a high place and showed him in an instant all the kingdoms of the world. And he said to him, "I will give you all their authority and splendor; it has been given to me, and I can give it to anyone I want to. If you worship me, it will all be yours." Jesus answered, "It is written: 'Worship the Lord your God and serve him only.'" The devil led him to Jerusalem and had him stand on the highest point of the temple. "If you are the Son of God," he said, "throw yourself down from here. For it is written: 'He will command his angels concerning you to guard you carefully; they will lift you up in their hands, so that you will not strike your foot against a stone.'" Jesus answered, "It is said: 'Do not put the Lord your God to the test.'" When the devil had finished all this tempting, he left him until an opportune time. Luke 4:1-13*

> *"Then I heard a loud voice in heaven say: 'Now have come the salvation and the power and the kingdom of our God, and the authority of his Messiah. For the **accuser** of our brothers and sisters, who accuses them before our God day and night, has been hurled down." Revelation 12:10*

c. Once we have taken the bait and are hooked, we become paralyzed. No matter how much the fish struggles…if the hook is in deep enough…the fish is on a fast track to the dinner table. Guilt paralyzes us, because behind guilt is fear. Satan uses our sin against us to destroy us.

> *"The thief comes only to steal and kill and destroy; I have come that they may have life, and have it to the full." John 10:10 NIV*

d. Unresolved guilt breeds more guilt. It doesn't just go away with time. If we don't deal with the existing guilt, the pain will many times cause us to run to sinful ways to escape the feeling of guilt. This will cause even more guilt and it "snowballs" from there if we don't deal with it.

> *"My guilt has overwhelmed me like a burden too heavy to bear. My wounds fester and are loathsome because of my sinful folly." Psalm 38:4-5*

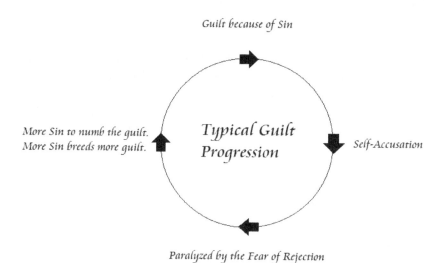

e. Once we have taken the bait, have been hooked really well, and find ourselves in bondage to our sin, our faith is neutralized: Faith is a basic principle of Christianity. It is impossible to walk in faith and guilt at the same time. Refusing to acknowledge and resolve our guilt is a form of unbelief. Because we are not accepting what God says in His word, "that if we repent we are forgiven," we choose to try to hide our sin and run from God, instead of running to Him for help. Only God can help us work through the resolution of guilt in our lives, so that faith can be restored.

6. Remedy for existential guilt

a. The worst thing that we can do is to run away from guilt. I must accept failure and that I fell into Satan's trap. We are in bondage to sin and we are helpless apart from God. We should confess our sin. To "confess" means to "agree" with God.

"If we confess our sins, he is faithful and just and will forgive us our sins and cleanse us from all unrighteousness." 1 John 1:9

b. We are not able to undo our sin unless God gives us the grace to repent, turn away, and change. To repent means to actually turn away from the sin, in other words, going in the opposite direction. Sometimes we don't want to repent. If we are not willing to repent, we should ask the Lord to bring us to repentance.

c. Make restitution (if possible). If you said or did something against someone, if at all possible, make it right. If we can't make restitution in person...sometimes the only thing we can do is to pray that God will heal the other person who was the recipient of our sinful behavior and ask Him to minimize the damage we have caused.

d. Allow God to build your character through this process. It is amazing how God is able to take our huge mistakes and use them to build our character and to make us stronger. But we must be willing to learn from our mistakes and make better choices in the future.

"For this very reason, make every effort to add to your faith goodness; and to goodness, knowledge; and to knowledge, self-control; and to self-control, perseverance; and to perseverance, godliness; and to godliness, mutual affection; and to mutual affection, love. For if you possess these qualities in increasing measure, they will keep you from being ineffective and unproductive in your knowledge of our Lord Jesus Christ. But whoever does not have them is nearsighted and blind, forgetting that they have been cleansed from their past sins." 2 Peter 1:5-9 NIV

7. Remorse versus Existential Guilt

a. Remorse avoids responsibility. Remorse is regret that we were caught or that bad things happened as a result of our choices, but not necessarily a true sense of sorrow that what we did was wrong.

1) Remorse comes out of our pride. Sometimes we want to try to make excuses or blame others for <u>our</u> actions.

38

2) There is no real resolution to it…we are stuck in the bitterness of the memory of what has happened. The word "remorse" comes from the Latin for *"torment"* and *"to bite"*.

3) Remorse in itself does not include repentance.

b. Existential guilt accepts responsibility. Guilt comes from God as a result of our sin. When we totally repent, we know that the sin has been dealt with.

> "Have mercy on me, O God, according to your unfailing love; according to your great compassion blot out my transgressions. Wash away all my iniquity and cleanse me from my sin. For I know my transgressions, and my sin is always before me. Against you, you only, have I sinned and done what is evil in your sight; so you are right in your verdict and justified when you judge. Surely I was sinful at birth, sinful from the time my mother conceived me. Yet you desired faithfulness even in the womb; you taught me wisdom in that secret place. Cleanse me with hyssop, and I will be clean; wash me, and I will be whiter than snow. Let me hear joy and gladness; let the bones you have crushed rejoice. Hide your face from my sins and blot out all my iniquity. Create in me a pure heart, O God, and renew a steadfast spirit within me. Do not cast me from your presence or take your Holy Spirit from me. Restore to me the joy of your salvation and grant me a willing spirit, to sustain me. Psalm 51:1-12 NIV*

> "Then I acknowledged my sin to you and did not cover up my iniquity. I said, "I will **confess** my transgressions to the Lord." And you forgave the guilt of my sin." Psalm 32:5 NIV*

> "I **confess** my iniquity; I am troubled by my sin." Psalm 38:18 NIV*

> "Whoever conceals their sins does not prosper, but the one who **confesses** and renounces them finds mercy." Proverbs 28:13 NIV*

> "Repent, then, and turn to God, so that your sins may be wiped out, that times of **refreshing** may come from the Lord. Acts 3:19 NIV*

> "Remorse speaks to the act, repentance speaks to the heart… remorse is an internal weight that follows as a result of wrong-doing. This feeling alone does not bring about correction." Dr. Mario Rivera*

JUST FYI

Judas and Peter – Remorse vs. Real Guilt

Judas, a Jewish zealot, betrayed Jesus for 30 pieces of silver. He was looking for a militant Messiah to save Israel from Roman tyranny. By conspiring with the authorities to arrest Jesus, he thought he could provoke Jesus to rise up against the Roman occupation and lead the armies of Israel into victory. His plan backfired and rather than revolting, Jesus went willingly to the cross to purchase our salvation. Judas, who was full of remorse because he miscalculated Jesus' agenda, realized Jesus wasn't the kind of Messiah he was looking for. He took the easy out and committed suicide. He couldn't deal with the shame of being wrong. He just wanted the pain and embarrassment to end but did nothing to remedy his guilt. He avoided responsibility.

Peter, on the other hand, also betrayed Jesus…not only once but three times. When the rooster crowed and Peter remembered Jesus' prediction that he would deny Jesus, he took responsibility for his actions, repented and wept bitterly. After His resurrection, Jesus found Peter out fishing, pulled him aside and ask him three times, "Peter…do you love me"? Then He gave Peter the command to "feed my sheep." Not many days after Jesus ascended into heaven, the Holy Spirit came at Pentecost and it was Peter who became the main spokesman for the Gospel message that was spreading like wildfire. Peter accepted responsibility, was restored and returned to become one of the key leaders in the early Church. Two men…two similar sins…two vastly different responses to guilt.

*****READ BEFORE STARTING*****

In order for you to complete the Theotherapy program all Study Questions and the Life Applications Sections must be completed and graded. Facilitators may grade Study Questions. The Life Application section will be reviewed by the group leader ONLY. Please don't hesitate to ask for help if needed!!!

Study Questions
1. What is the reason for existential guilt?
2. List the four things that happen in typical guilt development.
3. List the four things we need to do to remedy guilt.
4. What is the difference between remorse and existential guilt?

Life Application

1. Ask God to show you any place where you are experiencing existential guilt and why. If you would like to remedy this guilt follow the steps given in this chapter.
2. Write out 1John 1:9.
3. Share with us whatever you want to share about your experience.

MODULE # 8

NEUROTIC GUILT

Did you know?

1. Neurotic guilt is what is felt when one has no control over the situation and blames themselves for it.

2. Neurotic guilt is often a symptom of someone who blames themselves for everything that happens.

3. When someone experiences neurotic guilt it is often experienced with anxiety because we feel like everything is going wrong and everyone is mad at us.

4. Neurotic guilt is unfounded and shame-based. With neurotic guilt, there is no known reason for feeling guilty, we just "feel guilty all the time". We know something is wrong inside but we don't know what it is.

5. We feel that we must have done something wrong but we don't know what *it* is.

6. Some of us still feel guilty after we have followed all the steps to resolving existential guilt.

"Neurotic guilt refuses to yield to confession." Mario Rivera

Neurotic guilt and anger feel powerful. Fear feels helpless and weak. It is a way for us to think we are in charge of the situation. If we can punish ourselves by feeling guilty, we believe <u>we</u> have made atonement (payment). This is a form of control. We may think we don't need Jesus to be involved because we are taking care of the situation ourselves. We think that if we hurt badly enough, doing so should please God *(which is really making ourselves God if you honestly evaluate it).*

7. We develop the belief that *who I am* must be all wrong.

If we were not wanted as children, we feel guilty for existing. If we are always told we are bad, we begin to believe it and feel guilty. Neurotic guilt comes from the belief that I don't just do bad things, but that I am bad. If we are blamed when bad things happen we feel guilty.

    a. We lack a sense of well being, not knowing who we are outside of what we do. God is the only One who can correct this.

    b. As a result of past hurts and wounds which caused us to feel guilt, we continue to feel guilty when others express negative feelings; even if they have nothing to do with us.

    c. Repressed memories may cause paranoia and may be behind neurotic guilt. Experiencing childhood violence and abuse may have been too terrible to remember, and may not surface until we feel safe enough to face it.

8. Hindrances to restoration

    a. Neurotic guilt is shame producing. We may feel so guilty that we can't take feedback from others; we are so full of pain that we can't take another hit. Neurotic guilt says, "I don't deserve to be loved; I don't deserve to succeed."

    b. Neurotic guilt produces fear of punishment and also the belief that we deserve to be punished.

> *"But when the kindness and love of God our Savior appeared, He saved us, not because of righteous things we had done, but because of His mercy, He saved us through the washing of rebirth and renewal by the Holy Spirit, whom he poured out on us generously through Jesus Christ our Savior, so that, having been justified by his grace, we might become heirs having the hope of eternal life." Titus 3:4-7*

    c. We may feel neurotic guilt without knowing why we feel guilty or even being aware that we feel guilty.

    d. Neurotic guilt can be based in hidden beliefs (lies we believe) that cause us to feel hopeless and depressed so we keep repeating the same patterns over and over again. We may believe that if we change family patterns, (which may be neurotic yet still somehow "normal" or familiar to us), we will be in trouble or that we won't know how to act.

9. The resolution of neurotic guilt

   a. The cure for neurotic guilt is the application of the unconditional love of God. We need to feel loved and safe enough in order to talk about our neurotic guilt.

   "I have loved you with an everlasting love; I have drawn you with unfailing kindness."
   Jeremiah 31:3

   b. Resolving neurotic guilt may expose places where we have put others in the place of God (idolatry) and may also involve touching negative emotions. We may be so shattered that we need a lot of love to get free from neurotic guilt, and then be able to separate neurotic guilt from existential guilt.

   c. God provides a safe place where He can help us to discover where the guilt is coming from; and what events from our past are contributing to the neurotic guilt we are feeling.

   d. There is no hope inside the false belief system. Therefore, we need to ask God to begin uncovering the faulty belief system we have adopted from our dysfunctional family or significant others. We ask God to show us the truth. As we grieve the loss and see the truth, we can then be set free from the power of the lie and embrace the truth God has revealed to us.

      1) As we allow ourselves to receive God's love, we will see that even though we do bad things, through the grace of Jesus we are not condemned.

      2) As we receive God's unconditional love we begin to realize the truth about who we are and the truth about every situation that brought about the neurotic guilt.

3) We begin to realize that we are valuable because God sees us as valuable. We realize that our identity comes from God. Only He defines us.

"You have searched me, Lord, and you know me. I will praise you, Lord, with all my heart; before the "gods" I will sing your praise. You know when I sit and when I rise; you perceive my thoughts from afar. You discern my going out and my lying down; you are familiar with all my ways. Before a word is on my tongue you, Lord, know it completely. You hem me in behind and before, and you lay your hand upon me. Such knowledge is too wonderful for me, too lofty for me to attain. Where can I go from your Spirit? Where can I flee from your presence? If I go up to the heavens, you are there; if I make my bed in the depths, you are there. If I rise on the wings of the dawn, if I settle on the far side of the sea, even there your hand will guide me; your right hand will hold me fast. I say, "Surely the darkness will hide me and the light become night around me," even the darkness will not be dark to you; the night will shine like the day, for darkness is as light to you. For you created my inmost being; you knit me together in my mother's womb. I praise you because I am fearfully and wonderfully made; your works are wonderful, I know that full well. My frame was not hidden from you when I was made in the secret place, when I was woven together in the depths of the earth. Your eyes saw my unformed body; all the days ordained for me were written in your book before one of them came to be. How precious to me are your thoughts, God! How vast is the sum of them! Were I to count them, they would outnumber the grains of sand—when I awake, I am still with you." Psalm 139:1-18 NIV

*****READ BEFORE STARTING*****

In order for you to complete the Theotherapy program all Study Questions and the Life Applications Sections must be completed and graded. Facilitators may grade Study Questions. The Life Application section will be reviewed by the group leader ONLY. Please don't hesitate to ask for help if needed!!!

Study Questions
1. Name one hindrance to resolving neurotic guilt.
2. What is the cure for neurotic guilt?
3. Write Jeremiah 31:3

Life Application
1. Have you ever repented when you feel guilty and yet the guilt still remains? Explain. Which type of guilt are you experiencing?

MODULE # 9

ANXIETY

1. Origin of Anxiety

Anxiety was experienced for the first time in the Garden of Eden (Genesis 3). Imagine a world where there was no death, decay or deception. Imagine having a relationship with another human being that was so deep, so intimate and so transparent that you could look into each other's eyes without fear of rejection, disapproval or judgment. Imagine what it would be like to never worry, experience fear or have any sense of anxiety. Imagine what it would be like to be loved and cherished unconditionally, to never quarrel or to feel disappointed in each other. That's how it was in the beginning in the Garden of Eden.

When God created the universe, the earth and everything that exists on the earth, the Bible tells us that He saw what He had created and made the declaration that it was all *"very good."* It was absolute perfection without a single flaw. The same thing is true about the way Adam and Eve related to each other...perfectly and without flaw. They had everything they could possibly need or want. They lacked nothing. God's greatest gift to the first man and woman other than perfect relationship with each other and intimacy with Him was the freedom of choice...the freedom to choose to do good or evil...to love or to hate...to obey or disobey. God didn't want a bunch of programmed robots to love Him because they had been wired to do so...He wanted mankind to love Him because they desired closeness and intimacy with the God who created them.

In order to ensure that their freedom of choice was never taken from them, God also put a symbol of that choice in the Garden of Eden...the Tree of the Knowledge *(intimate experience with and understanding of)* Good and Evil. He told them they could eat of any tree or plant in the Garden...they just couldn't eat the fruit of the Tree of the Knowledge of Good and Evil without experiencing complete and total death and destruction to everything good they already knew and had experienced from the beginning.

Most of us know what happened next. Satan, disguised as a created animal tempted the couple to disobey God because Satan wanted them to think God was somehow deceiving them and withholding something they really needed to experience...the ability to be equal with God and to be as wise as the Creator. Eve was deceived by the Serpent and Adam who was with her willingly ate of the fruit they had been commanded to stay away from. The Bible tells us that immediately their eyes were opened and they saw the emptiness, the exposure and the vulnerability they now had. They were also immediately introduced to something new and sinister...guilt, fear and anxiety. As a result of the sin of disobeying God by eating from the Tree of the Knowledge of Good and Evil, Adam and Eve were guilty and felt ashamed, which caused them great anxiety. God drove them out of the safety and comfort of the Garden and into the cold, hard reality of the world. Every aspect of their lives would now be experienced through the feelings of fear, pain and anxiety...not because God was being unforgiving...but because their decision to disobey had brought about the disintegration of a guilt-free, anxiety-free life. In spite of their sin and disobedience, God still loved them, provided for them and even promised the plan of salvation for them that would eventually bring them back into intimacy and fellowship with God. But the ripple effects of their disobedience and sin would continue to haunt them for the rest of their lives. It would even continue to affect their descendants throughout history. We are those descendants...so we experience and feel the same things our ancestors did all because of the sin of disobedience.

2. Causes of Anxiety

   a. Anxiety comes when we are trying to be what we are not capable of being, or when we are trying to meet a need that we are not qualified to meet. Have you ever felt that feeling of panic when faced with having to accomplish something you feel absolutely unqualified to accomplish? It is a feeling we all have from time to time.

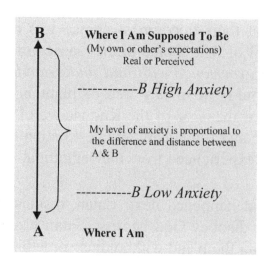

b. Some anxiety is good because it motivates us to accomplish things we need to accomplish. A certain amount of anxiety is what encourages us to go out and work so we can earn a paycheck to pay our bills and to provide for our families. A little anxiety also helps us to avoid procrastination in many areas of everyday life. However, constant feelings of strong anxiety that affect our peace or interrupt our sleep patterns are not healthy. When we have completed a certain task or accomplished a certain goal the anxiety should diminish. If, however, we live in a constant state of anxiety with no apparent resolution, we should take that as a *"red flag of warning"* indicating there is a deeper issue of fear that we have not fully dealt with.

c. Indecisiveness: when we are trying to make a decision but have mixed feelings about it (I want to...but I don't want to). It's like being stuck between a rock and a hard place. That inability to decide with confidence causes us to feel that uncomfortable feeling of unrest or even panic.

d. Fear of discovery: Have you ever been in a situation where you tried really hard to cover up what you had done or were really feeling because you were afraid that the "truth" would be exposed and that you would be vulnerable to rejection or abandonment? We experience anxiety and fear when we believe we will be exposed for who we really are, and because of our actions, failures or inability to perform according to what we think others will expect, they will reject us.

e. Basic insecurity or fear: The root of all depression, anxiety, and guilt is...you guessed it...fear. Feeling guilty is just a way for us to think that we are in control, almost like we believe we are actually doing something about the situation. As crazy as it may seem, we actually think that feeling guilty will make us feel less powerless...but it is just the opposite. Fear leads to neurotic behaviors which in turn cause feelings of guilt. We then try to medicate or numb out those feelings of guilt by engaging in more neurotic behaviors which in turn produce even more guilt. The vicious cycle just continues on and on.

f. Boredom: Did you know that anxiety can give us something to do when there is nothing else to do? Worrying about a situation also makes us feel that we are doing something about it even though worrying never really accomplishes anything of significance or value. Jesus encouraged us not to worry about tomorrow because each day has enough struggle of its own.

g. God's commandments become a place for anxiety because we know that apart from God's help, we cannot keep them. God knew we would struggle with that concept so He provided atonement (payment) for our failures through Jesus' sacrifice on the cross and also provided the Holy Spirit to comfort us when we fail, to empower us to choose correctly when faced with choices in life and to lead us into all truth in the process.

3. Levels of Anxiety

One of my favorite candies is peanut M&Ms. I just love the peanut encased in the layers of chocolate with the colorful candy coating on the outside. The peanut is at the core and then layers of other good ingredients like chocolate and that awesome hard shell candy coating are added to make it one of the greatest culinary delights imaginable…at least they rank at the top in my opinion.
Believe it or not…anxiety has different layers or levels just like the peanut M&M, although much of anxiety is unpleasant and not very fun to experience.

a. <u>Anxiety 1</u> – The foundation of the person is established in the first six years of an individual's life. Just like the peanut inside an M&M, Anxiety 1 makes up the core. When a child comes into this world, they have not yet developed the ability to cope with rejection, pain or trauma. Whatever negative things they experience early on in life become the core that all of their other later experiences add onto over time. So, if a child experiences deep rejection or trauma, it just stays there because there is no way for them to resolve it.

   1) The beginnings of that foundation or belief system generally take place in childhood or even in the womb.

   2) Early trauma leaves the child helpless with no opportunity to grieve or resolve losses. After that initial trauma, the layers begin to be added.

b. <u>Anxiety 2</u>- This is when circumstances seem bigger than they really are because new stresses compound and build on top of the anxiety already within.

   1) The addition of new "layers" of pain and trauma can begin anytime after the foundational anxiety has occurred. This secondary anxiety can develop even as a toddler.

2) These new layers can be caused by stressful and difficult living situations, relationship issues, abuse, conflict, lack etc. Anything that makes us feel powerless or inadequate. The layers just keep adding up.

"Humble yourselves, therefore, under God's mighty hand, that he may lift you up in due time. Cast all your anxiety on him because he cares for you." 1 Peter 5:6-7

3) Anxiety 2 is where most of us live our lives. In other words, we have core issues from our childhood that newer issues we experience as teenagers and adults have added to. We may have become very successful at "medicating" our feelings of anxiety through various addictions or behaviors, or by moving into denial and putting all of the pain from our childhood in a locked trunk somewhere in the back of our mind. We may even believe the old adage, *"out of sight, out of mind"*...kind of like the proverbial ostrich who tries to hide from danger with its head buried in the sand. Unfortunately for the ostrich...nothing has really changed. He is just as vulnerable as he was before he hid his head. Just like that ostrich, we cannot escape the reality of our childhood pain and anxiety by pretending it is not there. But that is what we tend to do...we pretend it isn't there and we can still function to a reasonable degree in spite of the unresolved trauma locked away in that trunk I referred to earlier. The only problem is that we are really fooling ourselves. The earlier trauma and pain is absolutely still affecting our choices, our relationships and our view of who we are and our place in this world.

4) Some of us will even resort to prescribed medications to help us feel less stress and anxiety. But the medication by itself usually just helps us cope with the symptoms and doesn't actually resolve the core problem...like just putting a Band-Aid on a deep wound that needs more than that to actually heal from the inside out.

c. Anxiety 3- This anxiety is like the colorful candy coating on the M&M only it doesn't taste good nor is it good for us. Anxiety 3 happens when the fear of dealing with everyday life circumstances begins to dominate our lives and relationships. We cannot function normally when we live in Anxiety 3. All of our "normal" or familiar ways of medicating or numbing away our pain no longer work. Anxiety 3 produces anxiety disorders.

1) At this level, all other anxieties we experience are expressed as phobias, addictions, etc.

2) Anxiety 3 can only be resolved by first addressing Anxiety 1 and 2.

"Do not be anxious about anything, but in every situation, by prayer and petition, with thanksgiving, present your requests to God. And the peace of God, which transcends all understanding, will guard your hearts and your minds in Christ Jesus."Philippians 4:6-7

4. How to get rid of anxiety or diffuse anxiety.

   a. Labeling - just knowing the source of our anxiety helps us feel less powerless. By honestly looking at our situation and our negative or neurotic reactions to our environment, we can then identify what is really going on within us. Doing so takes away some of the mystery of why we are so fearful. When things are brought out into the open or into the light, it feels less powerful and overwhelming. It's like turning on the light and seeing that the monster hiding under the bed is really something else...something that we still definitely need to deal with but no longer hiding under the cover of darkness and thereby keeping us in a place of fear.

      1) We should name the problem (What is my problem and what issue do I continue to struggle with?)

      2) We should name the feeling (what am I feeling right now?)

   b. Understanding the cause and learning how to let God deal with the root is the next step. According to Theotherapy Project alumnus Meggan Moon, God will give us:

      - Insights – *"Looking at the problem and developing theories about where it came from."*

      - Discernment – *"Determining which theory is really the correct one."*

      - Wisdom – *"Seeking out the answer using whatever resources are at your disposal (i.e. the Bible, another person, revelation through prayer, etc.)"*

c. Agape – the application of God's unconditional love

"Perfect love casts out fear." 1 John 4:18

1) As we see and accept how God loves us unconditionally, no matter what we have done, it will cause us to feel more secure.

2) Knowing that the all-powerful God loves and cares for me makes all my fears seem small and powerless.

Large Group Dynamic

Fall backwards and let someone catch you.
Have one person stand in the center of a circle of people with his/her eyes closed. Turn the person around several times and when they stop, have the person fall backwards into someone's arms.

*****READ BEFORE STARTING*****

In order for you to complete the Theotherapy program all Study Questions and the Life Applications Sections must be completed and graded. Facilitators may grade Study Questions. The Life Application section will be reviewed by the group leader ONLY. Please don't hesitate to ask for help if needed!!!

Study Questions
1. When does anxiety 1 begin?
2. How does anxiety 2 begin?
3. What is anxiety 3?
4. List three steps to resolving anxiety.

Personal Application
1. Finish this Sentence: I get anxious when…….
2. Can you think of a particular memory from your early childhood that comes back to your thoughts when you get anxious now?

3. Please write a letter to God sharing all of this with Him and read Psalm 139:1-18.
4. Share with us about how your have been able to resolve some of the anxiety you are feeling.
5. Let us know if you need help.

MODULE # 10

FEAR

1. We can all relate to what fear feels like. We all want to be in control of our situation and environment. It makes us feel safer when we think we have total control over what we experience. We don't like the feeling of being out of control so we tend to react in negative ways to that feeling of powerlessness. Did you know that road rage is really a manifestation of fear? People react in anger when they have been cut off or narrowly miss having an accident, or if they are afraid they will be late to where they are going and you are holding them up.

   a. Fear is a feeling of powerlessness in the face of someone or something greater or more powerful than us.

   b. All fear is based on:

      1) "You can take away something that I need to survive."

      2) "You have something I need and you may withhold it."

   c. Very small children believe their parents have this power. When you stop and think about it, small children are totally dependent on their parents for food, shelter, clothing…all of the basic things we need to survive. Without the parent's involvement, the child will die. The parents are bigger, stronger and have more knowledge than the child. Therefore, the child looks at the parents as being god-like. It's not until the child gets older that they can begin to understand the concept of an invisible God/Creator who loves them and has a wonderful plan for their life.

   d. As we mature, we come to know that only God has this power, and that our parents are not gods. We may love, appreciate and respect our parents in spite of their failures and imperfections, but we are no longer under any illusion that they have that kind of power in our lives.

   "When I was a child, I talked like a child, I thought like a child, I reasoned like a child. When I became a man, I put childish ways behind me." I Corinthians 13:11

   e. The emotionally mature person understands that God will never leave them nor forsake them.

"Can a mother forget the baby at her breast and have no compassion on the child she has borne? Though she may forget, I will not forget you! See, I have engraved you on the palms of my hands; your walls are ever before me." Isaiah 49:15, 16

"... I will never leave you nor forsake you." Joshua 1:5b NIV

"For I am convinced that neither death nor life, neither angels nor demons, neither the present nor the future, nor any powers, neither height nor depth, nor anything else in all creation, will be able to separate us from the love of God that is in Christ Jesus our Lord." Romans 8:38, 39 NIV

2. There are several types of fear that we would like to address in this module.

a. Fear of God

"The fear of the Lord is the beginning of wisdom, and knowledge of the Holy One is understanding." Proverbs 9:10 NIV

1) In reality, the only one we need to fear is God, and He has promised to be gracious to us. We are safe to feel powerless in His presence.

2) When we know Him for who He truly is…not who we have made him out to be based on our relationship with our parents or others who have hurt us, we will feel safe in knowing that He always has our best interest at heart.

"There is no fear in love. But perfect love drives out fear…I John 4:18

b. Other Fears

1) So where does fear come from? Believe it or not, there are only two fears we are born with. These are called innate fears and they are:

a) Fear of falling

b) Fear of loud noises

Have you ever been around an infant who gets startled by a loud noise or by being in the arms of someone who trips or loses their balance? The initial reaction is for the baby's eyes to get wide, their mouth to fly open and then after what seems like an eternity, they begin to wail. Their arms and legs shake, they ball up their fists and they won't settle down until they feel safe and secure again. They can't help it. It is a natural reaction to a lack of feeling safe. We are all born with these two fears and it takes training and experience to overcome these innate fears. I remember seeing old photographs from the turn of the last century where construction workers would be standing on steel beams with no safety harnesses hundreds of feet above the traffic below. These guys were not born with the ability to do that without fear. They had to learn to overcome it. The same thing is true for those who work around loud noises. They have learned to overcome their fear of the noise although they will still generally react when startled by a noise they aren't expecting.

c. Learned fears: When I was a small child living in Missouri I remember having an encounter with a small, white dog with brown spots named "Pooch-on". I was very young at the time so Pooch-on seemed bigger to me than he probably was in reality. He would sit on his porch and bark at people who would come by. One time I was walking down the sidewalk in front of Pooch-on's house and he came charging off of the porch with fangs bared and lots of barking and growling. If that wasn't enough to scare me, Pooch-on then chomped down on the seat of my pants and not only got my clothing between his teeth…he got some of my skin too! Needless to say, I was afraid of small white dogs with brown spots for a long time after that. It took me a while to overcome my fear of all small dogs. Sometimes I was more afraid of small dogs than I was afraid of large dogs. I wasn't born with that fear…it was something I learned through experience.

1) Unmet needs (fear of death, hunger, lack of shelter, pain, etc.). A small infant comes into the world with the expectation that they will be cared for by their parents. If a person's needs were adequately met as a child, there is no reason for them to fear that those needs won't be met as they get older. If, on the other hand, the child experienced want, lack or need, the child may grow up with a fear that their needs will not be met.

2) Basic insecurity (conditional love) - Children will be secure when they have experienced unconditional love in their family of origin. If, however, love was only expressed when they behaved perfectly, hit the homerun or received all A's on their report card, but instead were rejected if they didn't, the child will grow up with a performance mentality. They will only find value and worth if they get everything right. They may even transfer that same concept into their relationship with God. God is not like our parents. He loves us no matter what we do. In fact, He showed his love for us even when we rejected Him.

"But God demonstrates his own love for us in this: While we were still sinners, Christ died for us." Romans 5:8 NIV

"Once you were alienated from God and were enemies in your minds because of your evil behavior. But now he has reconciled you by Christ's physical body through death to present you holy in his sight, without blemish and free from accusation—" Colossians 1:21 - 22

d. Modeled fears - We tend to pick up the fears of those around us in our family of origin. Small children tend to be inquisitive and trusting unless given a reason not to trust. A child will not typically fear a mouse, for instance. If, however, the child observed mom screaming and jumping up on a chair every time she sees a mouse, it may cause the child to fear mice simply because of mother's reaction.

e. When our unresolved conflicts get the upper hand in our lives and we are doing nothing to resolve them in healthy ways, we may begin to move into deeper neurotic behavior. We may even develop phobias as a result of not dealing with our issues (or as one person I know puts it: "our frogs and lizards").

- A **PHOBIA** is an abnormal fear of an object that in itself is harmless, but in the mind of an individual it is threatening to his security and, therefore, causes fear. It may be a neurotic fear of heights, a fear of being under water, riding in an elevator, spiders, leaving the safety of the home or even the fear of peanut butter sticking to the roof of your mouth *(arachibutyrophobia)*. There are many kinds of phobias but beneath all of them is an extreme or irrational fear or aversion to something that would not normally be something that would affect us so deeply. (Read *Facing Unresolved Conflicts* by Dr. Mario Rivera, page 62-63).

f. Three Responses to Fear – the three F's: There are generally three responses to fear: **fight, freeze** and **flight**. When faced with a frightening situation, some people get aggressive and come out swinging while others may just freeze like the proverbial deer caught in the headlights. Still others may turn and run from the situation. Reactions like this can often be typical human behavior in a crisis. However, our responses to fear can also be influenced to a great degree by how we saw other family members react to scary situations.

g. Fear is at the root of much of our dysfunction. As we mentioned earlier, some anxiety is healthy and motivates us to accomplish things that are necessary for daily living in the real world. Anger in and of itself is not a sin...it is what we do with it that determines whether it is healthy or neurotic. Existential guilt is the guilt God uses to motivate us to turn from destructive behaviors and embrace His best for our lives. It is the kind of guilt that is easily remedied by confession and repentance. However, some anxiety, anger and guilt are neurotic and become the grid through which we see and experience life. In this context, anxiety, anger and guilt are not healthy. Fear is at the core of our neurotic anxiety, anger and guilt.

3. How do we diffuse fear?

"There is no fear in love. But perfect love drives out fear...I John 4:18

a. In order to diffuse fear it takes more than just "flipping your switch" and deciding not to be afraid. Fear can be a dark and debilitating force in our lives. We must own what we are feeling, come out of denial and take an honest look at where the fear is rooted. Sometimes we have constructed a view of our situation not entirely based in reality. Looking at it and actually separating the feeling from fact and the fantasy from reality can help us look at our situation with a more balanced perspective. Sometimes we may need others we trust to help point out errors in our judgment or thinking. When we keep things in the dark, it remains an unknown and therefore is full of mystery. That mystery gives fear a great deal of power in our lives.

b. Our basic fear comes from a false belief that we are alone, unloved and unprotected. The more we are able to embrace the truth that God is always with us, always loving us and always protecting us, the less we will be afraid.

c. When we get safe enough, we will be able to face what happened to us, bring it into the light and allow God to bring His healing for us into the midst of the grieving process.

4. Resolving ambivalence (conflicting emotions) - Ambivalence means having two conflicting emotions at the same time. Adults are generally able to see the good and bad in a situation or in another person. An adult understands that good people can still do very bad things just as bad people can sometimes actually do good things. Adults can also see the pros and cons of a specific situation. As a result of observing both the good and the bad, the adult can generally make the right choice in how to deal with the situation. A small child is not developed enough to understand these conflicting emotions. They see things as all good or all bad...not both good and bad.

a. Children will often try to remedy conflicting emotions in the parent.

    1) The child may develop contempt for self (because parents are all good, I must be bad if they say I am bad).

    2) The child may develop contempt for others (they hurt or frightened me so they must be all bad).

b. We can only effectively do this when we have owned our losses, identified the lies we have believed as a result of our losses, and have allowed God to make his presence known in the midst of our pain. He wants to show us the reality of what we experienced and He wants us to forgive ourselves and others for failing. We can only accomplish this with His help through the grieving process.

c. The results of resolving conflicting emotions are:

    1) It creates dependency on God because we know that He is ultimately in charge and that He has our best interest at heart.

    2) It works humility into us because we have to face our brokenness and come out of denial. We can actually come to grips with the fact that we have both strengths and weaknesses and that neither completely define us as a human being. We can feel safe to be broken in the presence of a holy and just God.

    3) It builds us up emotionally and brings deeper relationship with God because we are not so confused.

"A double minded (conflicted) man is unstable in all he does." James 1:8.

d. The refusal to deal with conflicting emotions causes us to live in constant fear and sets us up for:

    1) **IDOLATRY** – We tend to think of idolatry as the act of worshiping idols or images of wood or stone. We actually engage in idolatry anytime we have to look to others to make decisions for us or to tell us who we are. Whatever or whomever we put in God's place in our lives becomes an idol. We will put other things or people in God's place when we cannot trust Him with our pain.

    2) **HATRED** – Perfect love drives out fear. If we cannot accept God's perfect love for us in spite of our failures and brokenness, we may

come to hate either ourselves, or the other person who hurt or failed us. Self-hatred is the ultimate rejection of God's unconditional love for us.

3) **BITTERNESS** – If we do not deal with our anger, resentments and lack of forgiveness for those who have offended us, it will create a root of bitterness. That root of bitterness can become so deeply ingrained in our intellect that we cannot see the reality of the situation. We will continue to look at the world and at others through the grid of our wounding and dysfunction. We won't be able to get a completely accurate picture of what happened in our past or of what is currently happening in our present if we continue to see everything through the pain of our unresolved conflicts and emotional trauma. Failure to resolve our pain and an unwillingness to forgive those who have hurt us will stand in the way of us experiencing complete emotional freedom. We will not be able to see that God can and will turn it all around for good in our lives if everything we experience is seen through the lens of our unresolved pain and conflicts (Romans 8:28).

4) **RESENTMENT** – Resentment causes us to not want to be around anyone or anything that reminds us of the pain we have experienced, so we make no effort to resolve our conflicts.

"If your brother sins against you, go and show him his fault, just between the two of you. If he listens to you, you have won your brother over."
Matthew 18:1 NIV

"Get rid of all bitterness, rage and anger, brawling and slander, along with every form of malice. Be kind and compassionate to one another, forgiving each other, just as in Christ God forgave you." Ephesians 4:31,32 NIV

"And we know that in all things God works for the good of those who love him, who have been called according to his purpose." Romans 8:28

In order for you to complete the Theotherapy program all Study Questions and the Life Applications Sections must be completed and graded. Facilitators may grade Study Questions. The Life Application section will be reviewed by the group leader ONLY. Please don't hesitate to ask for help if needed!!!

Study Questions

1. All fear is based on what two things?
2. What are the two fears we are born with?
3. Define modeled fears.
4. What are three possible responses to fear?

Life Application

1. Complete this sentence, the thing I fear the most is......
2. Now try to connect the thing with something that took place in your early childhood.
3. Ask God to show you His presence in that memory.
4. Share with us about this experience.

MODULE # 11

Grief

1. **What Is Grief?** When we think of grief, we often think of the painful feelings we feel when a loved one dies. Have you ever been to a funeral and noticed the different ways friends and family of the deceased interact with each other? Some may be sitting alone crying. Others may seem to be in shock…they just can't believe this has happened. Still others may be angry at God that their loved one has passed away. You may even notice some who say things like "Why did God take them?" Some may be off in a corner laughing about good times remembered or funny stories about the person's life. You will see a lot of different emotions at a funeral. However, grief isn't just about funerals. Grief is a part of many other aspects of life. Grief is deep sorrow that is produced by *any* loss or pain - in order to be free from the pain, our losses <u>must</u> be grieved. The grieving process is the only way to resolve emotional wounds.

a. There are four basic kinds of pain:

1) Physical - Loss of health, comfort or strength in the body can produce tremendous grief.

Do you remember the actor who played *Superman* in the late 1970's? He was a very strong, handsome leading man in several different movies. After enjoying a great deal of success, his life was devastated by a terrible accident that left him completely paralyzed. In one horrible moment he went from being a person who could do anything he wanted anytime he wanted to do it…to a man who lived the rest of his life in a wheelchair and hooked up to a breathing apparatus. He couldn't even breathe for himself. I remember being very sad when I heard about the accident and very shocked when I saw him at his first public appearance after his accident. He talked very honestly about wanting to die when he found out that he would never walk or use a body part again. Over time, he was able to grieve his losses and find meaning to his life again.

2) Social - We all have a need to belong, so when we are rejected or removed from a group unwillingly, we are grieved and have a great sense of loss. Many people who are incarcerated feel a great deal of pain over being separated from their families. They can't hug their children whenever they want, go to their ball games or school events, or spend quality time with their spouse or other loved ones. That is a huge loss!

3) Emotional or Psychological - Emotional or psychological pain, and the loss of feeling loved or safe, can cause us so much grief that we become physically sick (psychosomatic illnesses). Not ever feeling safe is a big loss. Feeling alone and without someone to care for us is devastating.

4) Spiritual - Feeling the loss of harmony and communion with God is at the root of all of our problems. In order to grieve properly, we must ultimately forgive. Only God can work this forgiveness in our hearts.

b. Struggling with Ambivalence

1) Have you ever felt conflicted in a relationship or situation? Maybe you feel like you love someone and hate them at the same time. Ambivalence is having two opposite or contradicting feelings simultaneously. Sometimes we don't know what to feel...we just know that we hurt. You may even know someone you thought was close to perfect...but they failed you and broke your heart. Maybe someone cheated on you or took advantage of you and you now feel like you hate them with as much energy and passion as you loved them with. There is a fine line between love and hate. When we really love someone and they hurt us deeply, we can easily slip over the line and begin to feel that we hate them.

2) We need to resolve both good and bad feelings towards people in our lives. No one is totally good...and no one is totally bad. It is an adult characteristic to be able to see the good *and* bad in an individual. Sometimes we have a love/hate relationship with the people in our lives which can cause conflict within ourselves.

3) Children are not mentally developed enough to have two contradicting feelings at the same time. They see things as either all good or all bad. If a child is consistently rejected or wounded over a

period of time, he/she will most likely carry the inability to hold two conflicting emotions at the same time into his/her adult life. In order to change this dynamic, the child within, who is stuck, needs to grieve those losses incurred by the wounding.

c. Denial is our way of running from pain. We think that if we don't look at it or don't see it, then maybe it will go away. This is an automatic, God-given coping mechanism; however, we are not to remain stuck in denial. If the pain or loss was severe, sometimes we will have repressed memories, which God will surface as we feel safe.

2. God's method of dealing with loss

a. In the Bible, God models for us the proper way to deal with loss. He understands what it means to feel the deep loss and pain of rejection, abandonment, and of not being loved. The Bible tells us that Jesus was "familiar with grief (or the grieving process)". When we face rejection or loss and allow ourselves to own the pain and to feel all we need to feel emotionally, we call this the grieving process. The Bible tells us that:

"He was despised and rejected of men; a man of sorrows, and acquainted with grief: and we hid as it were our faces from him; he was despised, and we esteemed him not. Surely he had borne our grief, and carried our sorrows: yet we did esteem him stricken, smitten of God, and afflicted. But he was wounded for our transgressions; he was bruised for our iniquities: the chastisement of our peace was upon him; and with his stripes we are healed." Isaiah 53:3-5 KJV

b. We learn through reading the scriptures that the Lord Himself suffered loss and then grieved when sin entered the world. Sin always causes loss and it separates us from God. As we confess our sins and fully grieve what we have done and how it has affected others and ourselves, God meets us in that very vulnerable place to grant us forgiveness and emotional healing.

3. Stages of grief

a. **Shock/denial** - The first response we typically experience when faced with any loss is shock or denial. It is the way that God created us to react to any trauma. Just like your physical body goes into shock when you experience a serious physical injury and it takes a few moments for the pain to set in, so we also experience shock emotionally when we have been traumatized. Jesus himself expressed shock when the full realization dawned on him of what it meant to carry our sins to the cross and to experience God's wrath in our place.

"About three in the afternoon Jesus cried out with a loud voice, "Eli, Eli, lema sabachthani?" (which means "My God, my God, why have you forsaken me?")
Matthew 27:46 NIV

Even Jesus felt panic when faced with the heaviness, darkness and loneliness of being separated from God in order to pay for our sins. In spite of his great shock, he had already determined beforehand that he would complete the task no matter how frightening it was. That is why he said in a loud voice just before he died: *"It is finished! Father, into your hands I commit my spirit!"* The task was completed.

He was willing to face something no one else had ever faced in order to purchase our salvation.

"God made him who had no sin to be sin for us, so that in him we might become the righteousness of God." 2 Corinthians 5:21 NIV

Shock is a natural part of the grieving process; however, God does not want us to get stuck in shock because doing so causes us to remain in a place of denial. If we get stuck in denial, we aren't able to fully heal.

b. **Anger** - The next step in the grieving process is usually anger. Once the shock and numbness begin to wear off, we start to feel a sense of powerlessness...things happened outside of our control. That feeling of powerlessness causes us to feel angry. We don't like to feel out of control. It can be a very frightening feeling.

When we have experienced a serious physical injury, it sometimes takes a moment or two for the actual pain to begin to register in our brains. When the shock wears off, however, that's when the pain comes screaming in. Emotionally speaking, it is very similar. The pain of the event causes us to feel fear or frustration. This in turn makes us feel angry.

We tend to express anger in one of several ways. We may express it outwardly or we may internalize it. Remember, anger itself is not good or bad. It is just an emotion. What we do with it, however, is what determines whether it is a healthy or unhealthy expression of our anger.

1) Outward anger is expressed anger.

   a) Unhealthy outward expression – destroying property, hurting others, hurting ourselves, kicking the dog, punching your brother, cussing someone out, saying bad things about others, road rage, threatening others, doing violence are just a few examples.

   b) Healthy outward expression – hitting a punching bag, doing a role play with someone who can stand in for whoever you are mad at, running, jogging, exercising, rational confrontation, journaling, screaming into a pillow, using a sock bat on a chair, writing a nasty letter that you DO NOT mail! With the letter thing, say all of the things you wish you could say to the person you are mad at…get it all out…and then tear it up.

2) Inward anger is anger we internalize or hold inside. This can turn into depression, despair and self-destruction. There are many consequences to repressed anger…none of them are healthy. Even when we feel justifiable anger, it becomes sinful if we hold on to it or hurt others (or ourselves) in the expression of that anger. It will ultimately destroy us if we don't deal with it. God has given us a free will, which gives us the power to destroy our life or allow God to save it.

3) Processing through our anger is healthy if we do it in healthy ways. If we get stuck in anger, however, it can lead to rage, violence, rebellion, hatred, malice, slander, deeper depression, etc.

   • By the way, Jesus got angry on many occasions. You can read about it in the Scriptures. There were many times he expressed anger at the foolishness of his followers, or at the stubbornness of the religious leaders, or at the demonic realm that was continually seeking to destroy mankind.

c. **Sadness** - The next stage in the grief progression is sadness. Sadness comes as a result of facing the reality of what happened and what I actually lost as a result of the experience or trauma. It is allowing me to face the fact that things are different, and that I am missing what I lost.

Have you ever had a good cry? There's something about crying deeply that tends to take some of the energy out of our pain. Sometimes crying significantly can feel as cleansing and refreshing as the sky after a thunderstorm. It is the way God created us to express our sadness. Can you imagine what it would be like if we had all of these bottled up sad feelings and no way to let them out? When we get stuck in sadness and don't process on through it, it can become even deeper depression and can even lead to deep despair. When we get to that point, we begin to totally give up. People may get suicidal at that point because they just feel there is no resolution to their pain.

Yet, God as our divine Creator came up with the idea of crying to help us deal with sad feelings. Jesus himself knew about pain and sadness. Do you remember the story of Jesus' good friend Lazarus (John 11)? Jesus used to hang out with Lazarus and his two sisters Mary and Martha. He felt right at home in their house in Bethany and loved to be with them whenever he was in town. Once when Jesus was in another town preaching the Good News, Lazarus suddenly became deathly ill. His sisters knew who Jesus was and knew he healed sick people all the time. They sent word to Jesus to come back to Bethany a.s.a.p. so Lazarus could be healed. Yet, Jesus did a strange thing. He purposely waited until he knew Lazarus had been dead for four days. Jesus had a plan that would bring glory to his Father and would also be the catalyst in helping quite a few people find relationship with God as a result of the miracle he would perform.

When he finally did come in response to the sisters' request, he came with a plan knowing full well that very soon Lazarus would be raised from the dead and that all of his friends and loved ones would go from mourning to dancing! Even knowing all of this, when Jesus came to his friend's tomb, the Bible says:

"Jesus wept." John 11:35 NIV

He was still overcome with grief over the pain caused by sickness and death in the life of his friends and loved ones. He still felt the loss and grieved accordingly even though he knew it would all turn out alright in the end.

d. **Bargaining/Magical Thinking** - In this stage of grief we begin with the "what ifs". We might say, *"If only I had done something different, then this horrible thing would not have happened, or it could be changed."* Jesus understood this aspect of the grieving process. When he was

67

awaiting his own arrest in the Garden of Gethsemane...Jesus thought about possible alternatives to arrest and crucifixion and even asked his Father to consider if it could be accomplished another way. Yet, in spite of his very human need to bargain, he still chose to do his Father's will over his own and was triumphant on the cross.

"In your relationships with one another, have the same mindset as Christ Jesus: Who, being in very nature God, did not consider equality with God something to be used to his own advantage; rather, he made himself nothing by taking the very nature of a servant, being made in human likeness. And being found in appearance as a man, he humbled himself by becoming obedient to death—even death on a cross! Therefore God exalted him to the highest place and gave him the name that is above every name, that at the name of Jesus every knee should bow, in heaven and on earth and under the earth, and every tongue acknowledge that Jesus Christ is Lord, to the glory of God the Father." Philippians 2:5-11 NIV

If we get stuck in bargaining, it can become magical thinking. Magical thinking is a much deeper form of denial. Magical thinking involves a disconnection with reality and is very unhealthy.

e. **Forgiveness (Resolution)** is the final part of the grieving process. Unlike the other parts: anger, sadness, etc., forgiveness is not an emotion. It is an action...a choice of the will. The feelings must be expressed before the action can take place with any real resolution. True forgiveness from the heart will cost something. In order to truly forgive from the heart, we have to give up the idea that the person who hurt us will ever be able to make it right. We have to die to the idea of making them pay for the hurt they have caused us. Forgiving from the heart means we surrender the need to constantly remind them of how they hurt us. Forgiveness is truly experienced when we forgive in the midst of our pain.

As Jesus hung on the cross, He faced His greatest pain and emotional trauma. In the midst of His great loss and sacrifice, He chose to forgive. This act of forgiveness provided the way for <u>us</u> to be able to forgive and to walk free from the continual burden of loss and pain.

Forgiveness is the only way to get any resolution in the grieving process. If we choose not to forgive we will stay stuck in some or all parts of this process.

Warning: The refusal to advance through the stages of grief can result in low-grade depression.

4. Sometimes grieving may be delayed.

    a. It is essential to be in a safe place in order to fully grieve. It takes some work and some focus to be able to get vulnerable enough to fully grieve our losses. Safety is critical when it comes to fully resolving our emotional conflicts. We have to know that we are loved unconditionally and that those around us understand our pain and have our back. People who live in an abusive situation do not typically have this sanctuary.

    b. Delayed grief has painful side effects: relationship problems, chronic anger, fear of rejection, lack of motivation and depression.

    "When the pain of staying the same becomes greater than the pain of changing – we change!" Dr. Mario Rivera

5. Dealing with grief

    a. When a person gets "stuck" in grief, it becomes pathological grief.

    pathological – path-o-log-i-cal - involving, caused by, or of the nature of a physical or mental disease.

    1) Signs of pathological grief:

        a) The quality of life is below normal - it takes a tremendous amount of energy to suppress grief and to avoid dealing with it. Believe it or not…we have to work harder to push grief down than we do to express grief. Remember, God designed us to deal with pain by grieving and resolving it. If we choose <u>not</u> to "go there" or deal with it…it will begin to take its toll on every aspect of our lives.

        b) Absence of normal mourning – when we have pathological grief, there is no emotion felt or expressed when talking about, or experiencing really "bad stuff." We have learned to "successfully" push it to the back burner so we don't have to deal with it. The only problem is…not dealing with it leaves it all in a perpetual state of limbo and nothing about our situation really changes. Believe it or not, people can live their lives with emotional pain constantly beneath the surface because they have learned to accept the pain as "normal" or as a fact of life. They also may have a disconnection from being able to feel anything even when others are hurting.

c) Lingering depression - everything in life is drudgery and seems hopeless. It is like having a black rain cloud over your head or a lingering sense of heaviness or doom.

d) Psychosomatic problems - the body starts to experience pain and illness because of pent up emotion. The immune system becomes weak due to the emotional stress and therefore becomes more susceptible to illness.

e) Disorientation – Have you ever dealt with something so heavy or painful that it dominates your every waking moment? Did you notice that you may have found yourself forgetting something you were doing or just not being able to concentrate on anything? When this occurs, you start to forget a lot of things, and you just can't seem to get organized.

f) Personality change - this is a disruption in your emotional life that causes you to not act the same as usual. People with pathological grief have a very difficult time relating to others. They are consumed by their pain and therefore cannot connect with others who are not in the same situation. They may lose any sense of humor or joy. They may be incapable of seeing someone else's pain because their pain is so huge that it dominates every aspect of their life. They may show very little patience for those who are not "suffering" as they are. They may become very self focused.

g) Severe undiminished guilt – loss of interest in life/activities. The person with pathological grief may not be able to connect with everyday life situations and may have little motivation to step out of their current state of mind in order to even connect with close friends and family.

h) Phobic disorders (Read *Facing Unresolved Conflicts*, by Dr. Mario Rivera Page 62-63).

b. Expressing anger is a part of resolving grief; however, unresolved anger often becomes depression, which is another sign of pathological grief.

c. Remember, there can be no deep and lasting healing without a genuine expression of feeling and a corresponding change in your belief system.

d. There are several tools we can use to help us get in touch with our grief. Some of them are:

1) Role play – This is when we share our situation with someone we can trust by having them stand in for the persons who hurt us or for the persons we have hurt or relationships we have lost. The good thing about role play is that you get to be as angry or sad as you want to be with the person who is doing the role play with you and you don't have to worry about it offending them because they know it's not really about them. It is about your painful memory. You may be surprised at the amount of relief you can feel just by saying all of the things you always wish you had said but were afraid to. After really letting them have it…decide with your will that you will forgive them…not because they deserve it…but simply because you have the power to do so and because it is commanded by God.

2) Give voice and validity to your anger and pain by using a sock bat or by punching a pillow. You can really let it rip with this dynamic. The cool thing about it is that you can let go of a lot of emotional baggage without hurting anyone in the process. Believe it or not…you will feel much better. Diffuse guilt by forgiving yourself and others. Express anger in a safe manner. This is a necessary part of the grieving process.

3) After we express our anger, we must then release and let go of it. It is important to release our anger toward:

a) God - It is important to realize that much of our anger is actually toward God. Even though He doesn't deserve our anger, He understands why we feel the way we feel and He would rather us deal with it honestly than pretend it is not there.

b) Self - our anger towards ourselves can easily turn into self-hatred which is very harmful.

c) Others - we must release and let go of our anger toward others.

JUST FYI

Role Play…

The term role-play according to *The Cambridge International Dictionary of English* is defined as: **a method of acting out particular ways of behaving or pretending to be other people in order to teach people how to deal with new situations**. In the Theotherapy setting, trained facilitators use role-play as a tool for helping people recognize and "process" their emotions with the goal of bringing their unresolved conflicts to resolution.

Using role-play often helps a person gain access to deeper (repressed) emotions. In doing so they become more aware of how negative emotions have affected their lives and they can then resolve them.

6. Christian Fellowship

One thing that will help us deal effectively with grief is to have a good support system. Fellowship with other emotionally healthy believers is a vital part of your Christian growth and experience. You can give what you have received by becoming a safe person for others to be able to share their grief with.

In order for you to complete the Theotherapy program all Study Questions and the Life Applications Sections must be completed and graded. Facilitators may grade Study Questions. The Life Application section will be reviewed by the group leader ONLY. Please don't hesitate to ask for help if needed!!!

Study Questions
1. What are the four basic kinds of pain?
2. Why did God grieve?
3. List the five stages of grief.
4. What is pathological grief?
5. What causes psychosomatic problems?

Life Application
1. Name a significant loss you experienced in your childhood.
2. How did that loss affect you?
3. How did you feel about that loss?
4. Allow yourself to feel what you are feeling about that loss.
5. Ask God to show you the truth.
6. Ask Him to heal the pain and to comfort you.
7. What losses have you never fully grieved? What stage of the grieving process do you think you are stuck in?
8. What psychosomatic problems have you experienced?

MODULE # 12

SELF-ESTEEM AND MASKS

Let me ask you some honest questions: Do you feel that you have a high self esteem or a low self esteem? Do you feel awkward around people most of the time or are you pretty confident in most situations? Are you really shy around new people or do you act pretty much the same as you do around people you know well? Do you worry that people are judging you when they meet you for the first time or do you not really care what they think? Do you need others to say certain things to make you feel good about yourself?

When we have good (positive) self-esteem, we no longer need to look to others to meet our needs and tell us who we are, because we do not feel so empty inside.

One of the things we talk a lot about in Theotherapy is the idea of being "authentic". The way I like to define the word "authentic" is when we can own our strengths and weaknesses equally because neither define us as a person nor do they determine our sense of worth to God. When you know who you are, you can accept compliments without letting it go to your head. You can simply say "thank you" when someone compliments something you do well because you know that your skills or abilities do not determine your sense of worth or your value as a person. Conversely, you can accept constructive criticism about your weaknesses or failures without having to hide, deflect or become defensive because you know that your weaknesses and failures don't define you as a human being nor do they determine your worth or value as a person. When confronted with a weakness, you can simply say, "You know…you are right….that is an area I'm working on and need to grow in." No muss…no fuss! It is what it is. When you know who you are, you don't need others to say or do things to make you feel good about yourself.

1. Self-Esteem

   a. Self-esteem is how we see ourselves, and the value we apply to ourselves as a human being.

   b. Self-esteem is how we evaluate our self as a person according to our belief system. Remember those building blocks from Module 1? Our self-esteem is formed by our belief about ourselves in childhood. This is developed as we interact with others, particularly our parents, and other significant relationships in our lives. The family dynamic we grew up with has a great deal of influence on our self-esteem.

c. If we have a high self-esteem, we will be more secure in who we are as a person. High self-esteem is the ability to recognize and feel comfortable with both our weaknesses and our strengths. We can acknowledge our weaknesses and desire to change them. We can embrace our strengths and be comfortable with building on them because neither our strengths nor our weaknesses define us as human beings.

d. When we have a high self-esteem, we don't have to hide who we are. This gives others more freedom to be who *they* are without feeling insecure around us. Have you ever been around someone who just seemed to be at peace living their life? You noticed that they didn't take themselves too seriously. They could laugh at their mistakes and didn't have to toot their own horn about their successes. You may have felt really comfortable around them because you didn't feel judged by them. When someone knows who they are, they can risk being authentic and they don't feel the need to be critical of others.

2. Self-image

a. Self-image is how we think *others* view us. Our self-image comes from how we think others perceive us…what they think about us. Do you spend a lot of time wondering what others think about you? Do you feel insecure unless others are talking about how great, beautiful, talented, strong or wonderful you are?

b. If we have a low self-image, we will form a mask to cover and hide, so that the "real" us will not be exposed.

c. When we are uncomfortable with who we are, we may experience the following:

1) Fear of being discovered for who we think we really are, which only heightens our anxiety.

2) We may find ourselves expending great amounts of psychological energy just to live life.

75

3) We may feel the need to always be right because we are trying so hard to validate ourselves.

4) We may have a real fear of rejection. *"If they saw the real me, they would leave me or reject me."*

3. Causes of low self-esteem

a. The foundations of self-esteem are laid early in life. A child learns to trust or mistrust during infancy (first year). This trust in a parent will establish autonomy, or a sense of separation from mother (significant other).

> **au-ton-o-my** *noun – the right or condition of self-government; freedom from external control or influence; independence*

b. Interpersonal relationships play a major part in our development (especially in the fundamental unit-family). In bonding to our mother (significant other) a child will feel safe and loved. Apart from this very necessary bonding, a child develops a sense of shame for existing, or feels too unimportant to exist.

1) A child mainly bonds with their mother in the first couple of years of life. This gives the child the sense that it is good to exist even though the child has nothing to offer but their presence. A child cannot mow the lawn, cook a steak or work a job. All they can do is eat, sleep, cry, laugh, soil their diaper…and that's about it.

2) When a mother nurses her child, she isn't usually up cooking dinner or doing housework. She generally tends to sit down with the child in her arms and spends time connecting with her baby. The child's face is close to the mother's face so they can gaze at each other. The child receives nourishment from the mother's breast and feels the mother's heart beat. All of this reinforces a sense of peace and belonging in the child's psyche. It helps the child feel that they have a purpose for being…and that they belong.

3) At about 3 to 5 years of age, the child begins to bond more with Dad. The father gives the child a sense of identity. In most cultures a child receives its father's last name. We also get our bloodline from our father. When the father bonds with his child successfully, the child will tend to be secure in their identity.

4) What the child perceives that the mother and father think of him/her in the formational years will determine a good or bad self image and will greatly affect what they think others will think of them.

 c. Self rejection leads to low self-esteem

  1) Children can learn to reject themselves if they are treated badly in a dysfunctional home. Children tend to think their parents are all good, therefore the child must be all bad if their parents communicate that idea through their actions and attitudes.

  2) A family system in which it is never safe to be yourself causes a child to have low self-esteem and self-image.

4. Self hatred produces the following problems:

 a. Depression – internalized and unresolved anger because the child has had no sense of belonging or identity.

 b. Anger – We want to be accepted and loved unconditionally. When we don't feel unconditionally loved, we may become angry. In a child's life, much of that anger will be directed at themselves. They have to blame someone, so they blame themselves when they are rejected or unloved.

 c. Lack of self-assertiveness – A child may lack the ability to be assertive in healthy ways because his/her self-esteem is so low. He/she may feel unwelcome and therefore may not make any move to protect self or to verbalize his/her needs.

 d. Judging and criticizing others – When we hate our self, we try to deflect some of that negative feeling onto others. It helps us feel a little less scrutinized…a little less like a bug under a magnifying glass. We may tend to judge or criticize traits in others that we see in ourselves.

 e. Affects interpersonal relationships - Low self-esteem will absolutely affect our relationships with others. We won't be authentic and we will wear masks to suit the situation. The only problem is, if people are around us enough, sooner or later they will see beyond the mask. You may have been around someone who is "fake". Low self esteem will cause us to be like the chameleon that blends into its surroundings. We may also tend to be unable to stand for our convictions or moral values simply because we want to fit in so badly. People who do that typically are not respected by anyone.

f.   It gives us a false concept of ourselves. We are incapable or may even refuse to see ourselves as God sees us. We may make what others think about us more important than what God thinks about us. We will have an inability to accept ourselves or others.

g.   We may develop ways to shield ourselves from emotional pain. Some of those ways include:

1) Withdrawing / isolating / "numbing out" / addictive behaviors

2) We may become dependent on others because of fear. Or, fear that people will always disappoint us may cause us to avoid relationships altogether.

5. Masks

a.   The origin of wearing masks comes from a desire to please others but feeling totally inadequate to do so. This comes from a lack of self-worth. We may believe that, *"If I behave in a way that pleases you, then you will like me."* We then form the mask we think others want to see. However, as we feel safe enough to drop these masks, we begin to discover the real us and find significance and value in who we are as human beings, created in the image of God.

b.   When we feel pressure to meet others' expectations, we develop suitable masks to meet the demand.

c.   We long for people to know and love the *real* us. However, people are never really sure of who we are when we wear masks, because our real self is hidden.

d.   Compliments feel uncomfortable, because we know others are praising our mask instead of the real us.

e.   Criticism hurts more than it should. We fear it is the real us, and not our mask being attacked, because we really do believe it is proof of our worthlessness.

f. Masks keep us from growing, because the Lord changes the real person, not the mask. Not only do we protect ourselves from being hurt, we also guard ourselves from receiving love.

g. Masks inhibit social interaction with others because a good relationship requires a level of intimacy our masks will not allow. This produces even more rejection and inhibits emotional growth.

h. We are set up for further rejection when our masks prove themselves to be inadequate.

6. Cure for Low Self-Esteem and Masks

a. Identify the masks – take an honest inventory of the ways we try to convince ourselves, others and even God that we are someone different than who we really are.

b. Recognize self-images that are contrary to the "real" self and choose to believe the truth of what God says about us.

c. As we look to God for our value and worth, we will no longer need to look to others to give us a sense of worth and significance.

d. Separate our worth from our performance and decisions. We need to know we are accepted unconditionally apart from our performance.

e. Discover value in the greatest significant other…the Lord! What He says and thinks about us is what ultimately matters. We can be safe to be flawed, broken and very human in His presence because He loves us unconditionally.

f. As we discover that the Lord is our significant other and not our parents, we will develop a good self-image, and will not need to set goals for ourselves based on others' expectations.

In order for you to complete the Theotherapy program all Study Questions and the Life Applications Sections must be completed and graded. Facilitators may grade Study Questions. The Life Application section will be reviewed by the group leader ONLY. Please don't hesitate to ask for help if needed!!!

Study Questions

1. What is self-esteem?
2. What is self-image?
3. What is the origin of masks?
4. List the six cures for low self-esteem and masks.
5. What are some ways a person defends themselves against psychological pain?
6. How can compliments be a problem if a person wears masks?

Life Application

1. Describe which of these two you relate to most and why:
   Low self-esteem
   Poor self-image
2. Describe at least two masks you have worn, how you thought they helped you, and how they hindered you.
3. Ask God to show you your real self. Choose to believe the truth about what God says about you.

MODULE # 13

GROWTH MARKERS - How you can tell if you are making progress in your journey to emotional freedom.

If I were to ask you how I could get from here to another city by car using the interstate highway…how would you tell me to get there? Once I was going in the right direction on the interstate, how would I know where I was at the moment, how much progress I was making, or where to go if I needed to stop to get some gas or a bite to eat? If you answered, *"by reading the road signs, exit signs and mile markers"*…you would be absolutely right! The way you can tell what kind of progress you are making on a particular journey is to pay attention to the signs along the way!

The same thing is true about the journey of emotional healing we have been discussing throughout this book. If we want to know what kind of progress we are making on that journey, we need to look at where we have been, where we are right now, and where we want to go. In this module, we will discuss growth markers; road signs to recovery and healing. There are many different growth markers and our individual journeys may differ…but here are some general signs to help you determine whether you are making real progress:

1. Seeing myself as a perpetrator instead of only as a victim. Learning to see where I have hurt others instead of focusing only on where I was hurt:

    a. The other side of evil in our lives is our own sin and the places where we have sinned against others.

    b. We should ask ourselves the question: where have I hurt, abused, or taken advantage of others? Let's take a moment to reflect on our own sin and what it has cost others.

    c. Repentance is when we confess our sin, turn from it and move in a totally different direction. Only God can bring us to total repentance. His goodness and His mercy lead us to want to change, and then He gives us the strength and ability to do it.

"Or do you show contempt for the riches of His kindness, tolerance and patience, not realizing that God's kindness leads you toward repentance?" Romans 2:4.

"Repent, then and turn to God, so that your sins may be wiped out, that times of refreshing may come from the Lord." Acts 3:19.

2. Recognizing self-sabotage:

   a. Self-sabotage is when a person continues to spoil or hinder his/her own success by constantly engaging in behaviors that hurt them.

   b. Some people are literally afraid of success and will hinder or destroy their own ability to accomplish good things in life because they fear the unknown.

   c. For some, the destructive cycle of addiction feels more familiar…even though we may hate it…so we will default to the old behavior because we feel we are in familiar territory.

   d. Sometimes we will set unrealistic goals for ourselves and then wonder why we couldn't reach those goals. If we want to succeed, we should:

      1) Set challenging yet realistic goals

      2) Learn to avoid the traps we tend to fall into

3. Developing a healthy self-esteem: Remember what we talked about in the last module? Self-esteem is how we see ourselves. In order to have a good self-esteem, we must learn to see ourselves from God's perspective. There is good and bad in all of us. God has a completely accurate view of us, yet He loves us unconditionally and never gives up on us.

   "And we …are being transformed into His likeness with ever-increasing glory, which comes from the Lord, who is the Spirit." 2 Corinthians 3:18

   "The heart is deceitful above all things and beyond cure. Who can understand it?" Jeremiah 17:9

   "I have loved thee with an everlasting love." Jeremiah 31:3 KJV

4. Learning to live out of God's love: In order to live out of God's love, we must first experience His unconditional love. It is impossible to give what

we have not received. As we receive God's love, we are then able to love others. As we love others, God pours more love into us.

"Jesus replied, 'Love the Lord your God with all your heart and with all your soul and with all your mind. This is the first and greatest commandment. And the second is like it: Love your neighbor as yourself'." Matthew 22:37-39.

5. Looking to God as our source for living life and loving others: Instead of constantly looking to receive acceptance and to be loved by others, we need to look to God for our love and acceptance, so that we can *give* to others. It is only as we let GOD supply us with love for ourselves that we can love and give to others.

   a. God is our true and all powerful resource for living. When we are not hooked up to God, we have nothing to give that can keep us spiritually healthy or that can effectively help others. We can only truly and successfully live life through a relationship with God, otherwise we will be doing it all in our own strength and will not be very effective.

   b. We should also ask ourselves the question: where have we used others? We must own how we have used others for our benefit. We must desire to give instead of always receiving. The Bible tells us that it is much more blessed to give than to receive. When we experience true and deep emotional healing, the natural by-product of that healing will be a genuine and heartfelt desire to help others experience healing as well.

6. Learning to separate who God is from who our parents are. Our parents are not gods and God is not like our parents. When we were young, our parents were the ultimate authority in our lives. However, as we mature, we continue to love and respect our parents for the role they played in our lives…but we learn to respect God as our ultimate authority and "Parent".

   • Anyone who has emotional control over us is a block to our ability to see God appropriately. When we look to God and see our parents instead, we develop a false image of who God is.

7. Identifying and dissolving double bind situations. These are no-win situations that cause conflict in our lives. We are faced with a difficult situation and either way, we may experience negative consequences as a result of our choices. We have to face the fear and do what is right. Someone once said that character is what we are when no one else is

looking. The more healing we get, the more we want to do the right thing whether anyone is looking or not.

8. Walking in who I am according to God's perspective:

a. It is the "real me" that can have true fellowship with God and others. When we find out that we are not as bad as we think we are, and that much of our life has been wasted trying to live up to a negative self-image because of our self destructive behavior, we can then allow God to give us *His* perspective for who He says we are.

> *"Now if we are children, then we are heirs, heirs of God and co-heirs with Christ..."*
> Romans: 8:17

> *"I have given them the glory that you gave me, that they may be one as we are one: I in them and you in me. May they be brought to complete unity to let the world know that you sent me and have loved them even as you have loved me."*
> John 17:22-23

b. When we believe we must always be bad, do bad things, and pay bad prices, we will tend to live out of those beliefs. However, when we start to agree with God that He loves us and has made us righteous, we can become transformed into His image!

c. Our childhood solutions become our adult problems. What worked for us as children is not working now. We can't keep blaming our dysfunction on others and thereby not taking the initiative to make any changes. We must stop expecting other people to change, and clearly recognize in ourselves what <u>we</u> need to change.

> "I don't have problems, I am the problem." (Read *Facing Unresolved Conflicts*)
> bottom of page 25 and page 26).

> *"When I was a child, I talked like a child, I thought like a child, I reasoned like a child. When I became a man, I put childish ways behind me."* 1 Corinthians 13:11.

d. We will know we are walking in greater healing and maturity as we see our reactions and attitudes towards self, others, and God change as we experience more and deeper emotional healing.

9. Learning to handle injustice with a broader perspective of the sovereignty of God:

   a. As we heal, we must learn to accept the frailty and rebellion of man. Why does God allow bad things to happen to people? God created us with a free will to make our own decisions. If we choose to do bad things and hurt others, He will not violate our will by stopping us. God has given us total freedom to save our lives or to destroy them. He will not take away our freedom to do so.

   b. Refuse to blame God for evil. God is good. God is love. Evil prospers is the absence of submission to God. The deceiver (Satan) tricks us into believing the lie that God is evil or that He doesn't have our best interest at heart. God is not evil but He can turn evil into good.

   "And we know that in all things God works for the good of those who love Him, who have been called according to His purpose." Romans 8:28 NIV

   "Come now, and let us reason together, saith the Lord: though your sins be as scarlet, they shall be as white as snow; though they be red like crimson, they shall be as wool." Isaiah 1:18 KJV

   "Once you were alienated from God and were enemies in your minds because of your evil behavior. But now he has reconciled you by Christ's physical body through death to present you holy in his sight, without blemish and free from accusation—" Colossians 1:21-22 NIV

10. Experiencing Love where there used to be fear. As we heal, we will begin to realize the truth that God is always with us at our worst.

"Be strong and courageous. Do not be afraid or terrified because of them, for the Lord your God goes with you, <u>He will never leave you nor forsake you</u>." Deuteronomy 31:6

   - It is the lies and deceptions we believe, that keep us from moving forward on our journey of healing. As we heal, we will gain more confidence in decision making - as more of the truth replaces our wrong thinking, we will develop more confidence to choose correctly and to make healthy decisions.

11. Refusing to run from feelings and pain. It is typical human nature to want to run from feelings and pain. The more we heal emotionally, the more we will begin to see that God is at work in the midst of our painful circumstances.

Rather than running to the old ways of dealing with pain, we learn to run _to_ God for comfort, wisdom and healing.

a. We begin to ask for what we need and to say how we feel.

b. We learn to pray and wait on God for His answer to our problems and for His glory to be evident in the process of working on us. As we learn to safely trust in Him for the outcome, we will find that He will not disappoint us.

c. We learn to add hope to faith and love. As we see how the Lord desires to change us, our hope will become greater. God will give us hope that He will turn evil around for good. When God is on the scene, there is hope.

   "Let us draw near to God with a sincere heart in full abundance of faith, having our hearts sprinkled to cleanse us from a guilty conscience and having our bodies washed with pure water. Let us hold unswervingly to the hope we profess for He who promised is faithful." Hebrews 10:22-23.

12. Moving away from self-destruction:

a. We learn to ask ourselves the question: "Who is doing _what_ to me?" Sometimes people _are_ doing "bad things" to us; but a lot of the time, we are doing "bad things" to others or we may be actively engaging in self-sabotage. The question is, "who is doing what?"

b. The more we heal, the more we come out of denial - only the emotionally mature person can look at themselves objectively. We often deny that we are the problem.

c. We learn to take responsibility - there are a lot of things that God has given us responsibility over. We should take responsibility for our own feelings, actions, behavior and attitudes. It is very important for us to remember:

"We don't have problems, we are the problem."

In order for you to complete the Theotherapy program all Study Questions and the Life Applications Sections must be completed and graded. Facilitators may grade Study Questions. The Life Application section will be reviewed by the group leader ONLY. Please don't hesitate to ask for help if needed!!!

Study Questions
1. What is self-sabotage?
2. How can a healthy self-esteem be developed?
3. According to Matthew 22:37-39, what are the two greatest commandments?

Life Application
1. Is self-sabotage an issue in your life? If yes, please give us an example.
2. What happens in your life when you start to walk in who God says you are?
3. Can you see yourself moving towards any of these growth markers? If so, what are they?
4. Which of these growth markers jump out at you the most, as something that needs to happen in your life?
5. Identify and explain a double bind you have experienced.
6. In what way/ways have you changed since studying Theotherapy?

MODULE # 14

COMMUNICATION

"In the past God spoke to our ancestors through the prophets at many times and in various ways, but in these last days he has spoken to us by his Son, whom he appointed heir of all things, and through whom also he made the universe. The Son is the radiance of God's glory and the exact representation of his being, sustaining all things by his powerful word. After he had provided purification for sins, he sat down at the right hand of the Majesty in heaven." Hebrews 1:1-3 NIV

From the very beginning of creation, God has longed for relationship with us and has wanted you and I to understand how important healthy relationships are for us. In the beginning, God made the declaration that, *"...it is not good for man to be alone...",* and he modeled that concept personally for Adam and Eve, the first man and woman. Not only did He show them individually what relationship with Him would look like, He also provided the way for them to have healthy relationships with each other and with others who would come along later…God with Adam, God with Eve, Adam with Eve, God with Adam and Eve as a couple, Adam with others, Eve with others, Adam and Eve as a couple in relationship with others.

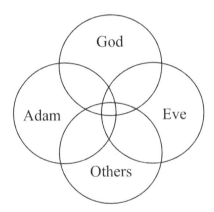

Everything was perfect in the Garden of Eden. Adam and Eve were able to walk and talk with God every single day and were able to understand what He wanted to communicate to them. However, when they disobeyed and sin entered into the picture (Genesis 3)…communication between Adam and Eve and their loving Creator began to break down.

Then the man and his wife heard the sound of the LORD God as he was walking in the garden in the cool of the day, and they hid from the LORD God among the trees of the garden. But the LORD God called to the man, "Where are you?" Genesis 3:8-9

From the moment "the fall of man" took place all those centuries ago, man's communication with God became more and more distorted. Sin and rebellion against God caused all kinds of interference in what mankind was hearing God say. God's message was always the same...it never changed...but man's ability to hear and understand God was severely diminished by the effects of sin. Sin brought distortion to every aspect of mankind's communication.

JUST FYI

Looking at distortion...

Remember those old transistor AM radios from years gone by? You had to carefully roll the tuning dial through all the static to finally get a clear signal from your favorite radio station. Our issues and conflicts cause distortion in our communication. Getting rid of the "distortion" helps us hear better and communicate more effectively. What are some of the things distorting your communication with others?

God was grieved that sin had entered into the world and that man could no longer hear His voice clearly. The distortion and static that came as a result of man's sinful behavior continually blocked man's ability to regain the place of intimacy Adam and Eve had originally experienced with God. So, throughout history, God would continue to speak to those who still had the capacity to hear Him. Great heroes of the faith like Noah, Abraham, Moses and others who chose to remain close to God and to live a different lifestyle from what their culture was living, still spoke with God and heard him clearly. As the centuries rolled by, God spoke through prophets like Isaiah, Jeremiah, Hosea and others, continually calling out to mankind to return to fellowship and intimacy with Him. Some heard what the prophets were saying and returned to God. Most of mankind, however, continued to allow the distortion of sin to inhibit their opportunity to have true relationship with their Creator.

The Bible goes on to tell us that at just the right time in history, God Himself came to this world in human flesh to not only tell us...but to show us what God was really like...not what society had made Him out to be.

But when the set time had fully come, God sent his Son, born of a woman, born under the law, to redeem those under the law, that we might receive adoption to sonship. Because you are his sons, God sent the Spirit of his Son into our hearts, the Spirit who calls out, "Abba, Father." So you are no longer a slave, but God's child; and since you are his child, God has made you also an heir. Galatians 4:4-7

Jesus answered: "... Anyone who has seen me has seen the Father..." John 14:9

"I and the father are one..." John 10:30

Jesus gave them this answer: "Very truly I tell you, the Son can do nothing by himself; he can do only what he sees his Father doing, because whatever the Father does the Son also does. John 5:19

God sent his only Son Jesus to show us exactly what God is like and to show mankind His heart for restoring the intimacy that was lost in the Garden of Eden due to Adam and Eve's choice to disobey God.

God actually created us for relationship. Effective communication is the way this happens. It is important for us to learn how to hear and how to speak so that we can communicate accurately and clearly. Effective communication will produce healthy relationships. God desires for us to learn how to effectively communicate.

Jesus said, *"My sheep listen to my voice; I know them, and they follow me." John 10:27*

1. Components of Communication

We communicate by words, and actions, tone of voice and body language. Jesus' behavior and words were always in agreement. His words always matched His actions and He is our example. Effective communication has three main components:

    A. **SENDER** – The sender has a message that he/she sends with his/her words and actions.

    B. **MESSAGE** –The message is what the sender is trying to get across (communicate).

    C. **RECEIVER** – The receiver trics to hear what the sender (message) is saying.

2. Rules of Communication

    A. It takes at least two people to communicate.

    B. We are always communicating, either with our words or with our actions. Only 7% of communication is verbal, the rest is communicated by how we behave (body language, tone of voice, facial expressions, etc).

3. The angle of distortion

Our communication problems are based on distortion. Just about every problem mankind encounters in his relationship with others has to do with miscommunication. Wars have been fought, relationships have ended badly, marriages have broken up...often simply because of distortion in our communication with others. No one except Jesus can perfectly and consistently send and receive completely accurate messages. The rest of us hear and speak based on our way of understanding. The grid through which we look at life is called *"the angle of distortion"*. Remember the Negative Active Past we talked about in Part 1? Our NAP is a big part of the grid through which we look at life and relationships. Our past wounds, traumas and the lies we have believed due to our sin and the sins of others against us absolutely color the way we communicate. Just because I say something doesn't mean I have been understood.

What all of us hear is based upon our:

Perception + opinion = distortion

    Perception – a way of understanding or interpreting something.
    Opinion- beliefs or views about something not necessarily based on fact.
    Distortion- a misleading or false account or impression; twisted

It takes a great deal of emotional healing to be able to see things from another person's perspective. We may actually be wrong sometimes in what we perceive about the situation we are in and what the other person may be saying. Sometimes we spend a great deal of energy trying to figure out what the other person meant by what they said. When in doubt, we should ask the other person what they meant or reflect back what we "heard" them say so they can clarify their position rather than us just assigning motive to their communication. We get into trouble when we project motive onto someone else.

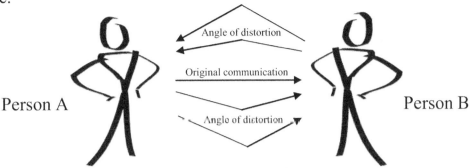

In the illustration above, Person A started off with the original communication that he thought was totally clear and direct. Person B reacted based on his perception of what he thinks he heard Person A say. Person A then reacts to Person B's reaction. Each time they react, the angle of distortion becomes greater because the original message is becoming lost due to both Person A's and Person B's "grid" based on their individual NAP.

4. The process of communicating

From the time we are born, we develop our own beliefs based on what was communicated to us. All that we have perceived comes into all of our conversations. For example, when someone says, "I love you", we all "hear" a different message based on our past experience. That statement could produce a good, bad, or indifferent feeling within us, which will affect how we "hear" what people mean when they say "I love you" today.

5. Types of communication

Remember…only 7% of what we communicate is the actual words. The rest of our communication is through body language, tone of voice, facial expression, etc.

A. Just the words (digital communication)

1. Printed or written words alone are insufficient for talking about relationships. Unless you know the person extremely well that you are communicating with…it is basically up for grabs as far as what that person thinks you are saying. If you look at different forms of communication like emails and texting, technology has given us "emoticons" (emotion + icons or pictures) to help us communicate the heart or feeling behind the communication. ☺ (See what I mean?)

2. Relationship is obtained through communicating your heart, which requires words, feelings and expressions.

B. Non-verbal (analogical communication)

1. Communicating through our body language (facial expressions, tone of voice, etc.) can make a huge difference in how others read and understand our communication. It has been said that the body does not lie. You can say one thing with your mouth (your words) but your body will tend to communicate what is really going on with you. You have heard it said that "a picture is worth a thousand words." That really is true because people will evaluate our communication based on the whole enchilada…not just by what we say. People can tell whether or not we are being genuine and authentic by watching to see if our words, actions and body language match.

2. Behavior is non-verbal communication and is what defines the relationship with another person. If you say you care for someone but treat them badly or act impatient with them…all the words in the world will not mask what is really going on inside of us.

We believe what people do…not just what they say.

C. God communicates to us in various ways…through His Word (the Bible), through His creation and through our circumstances. You can't put God in a box and He will use whatever means necessary to get our attention. The greatest example of God communicating His love for us is when Jesus Christ hung on the cross. By sacrificing His life for us and paying the penalty Himself for our sin, God "showed" mankind clearly that His love for us is unconditional, redemptive and of unfathomable value. Jesus words and behavior always matched. He has given us the ability to communicate clearly and truthfully as we receive His healing in our lives.

JUST FYI

Miscommunication of "Titanic" Proportions....

The British ship *RMS Titanic* sank at 2:20 AM on April 15th 1912, after colliding with an iceberg just before midnight on April 14th. 1,517 souls were lost as the great "unsinkable" ship broke in half and sank beneath the waves. It was one of the most devastating maritime disasters in recorded history. This huge loss of life was not as much about hitting an iceberg or having too few lifeboats as it was about a tremendous breakdown in communication.

Wireless operators Jack Phillips and Harold Bride were busy sending out the international distress signal (called a CQD at that time). Several ships responded, including *Titanic*'s sister ship, *Olympic*, but none was close enough to arrive in time. The closest ship to respond was the *Carpathia*, which was 58 miles away. Traveling at top speed, it could only arrive in an estimated four hours—too late to rescue all of *Titanic*'s passengers.

From the bridge of the *Titanic*, the lights of a nearby ship could be seen in the distance. Historians believe it was probably the *SS Californian*. Whatever ship it was, it did not receive *Titanic's* frantic wireless communications so crewmembers aboard the sinking ship attempted to signal the ship with a Morse lamp and distress flares. Sadly, the other ship never appeared to respond.

The *Californian*, which was nearby and stopped for the night because of ice, also saw lights in the distance. *Californian*'s wireless was turned off, and the wireless operator had gone to bed for the night. However, just before he went to bed at around 11:00PM, *Californian*'s radio operator attempted to warn *Titanic* that there was ice ahead, but he was cut off by an exhausted Jack Phillips, who had fired back an angry response, "Shut up, shut up, I am busy; I am working Cape Race", referring to a solitary Newfoundland wireless station that had received *Titanic's* distress call. When *Californian*'s officers first saw the ship, they tried signaling her with their Morse lamp, but also never appeared to receive a response. It was too little too late. By the next morning, over 1,500 people had needlessly perished as a result of poor communication.

Not long ago, I saw a television documentary about further exploration of the *Titanic* wreck site. The program showed videos from a deep sea robotic camera as it wove in and out of the ghostly cabins and staterooms. As it came into the communications room where the Marconi Telegraph equipment was located, the camera zoomed in on the power switch Jack Phillips was in charge of that fateful night. True to history, the power switch was in the "off" position with the headphones resting neatly right where Phillips placed them almost 100 years ago.

*****READ BEFORE STARTING*****

In order for you to complete the Theotherapy program all Study Questions and the Life Applications Sections must be completed and graded. Facilitators may grade Study Questions. The Life Application section will be reviewed by the group leader ONLY. Please don't hesitate to ask for help if needed!!!

Study Questions

1. What is communication?

2. What are the three components of communication?

     a.

     b.

     c.

3. What is the angle of distortion?

Life Application

1. What communication patterns can you identify in your life?

DYNAMICS MODULE #14:

1. Be completely silent (no talking) for two minutes. What sounds did you hear?

2. Look into the eyes of a partner for two full minutes without speaking. What did each of you see or what impressions did each of you have during the exercise?

3. Pair up with a partner and while one is talking, the other is to listen without talking (the listener can indicate with their body language that they are hearing and comprehending…but no words are to be spoken by the listener). Then switch. What was communicated?

MODULE # 15

FAMILY SYSTEMS

"Train up a child in the way he should go, and when he is old he will not turn from it."
Proverbs 22:6 NIV

1. Rules of the family

Every family, regardless of how functional or dysfunctional it may be, has a set of rules the family members learn to live by. Many of these rules are spoken rules because the rules are reiterated verbally, but some family rules are unspoken and are learned by experience within the family unit over a period of time. Here are several types of family rules:

A. There are dysfunctional and sick rules that can be carefully passed down from one generation to the next. Some examples of dysfunctional rules are:

> 1. Don't show negative emotion. Feelings of anger, sadness, disagreement with unfair discipline or a difference of opinion are invalidated or punished. In some families, the parents are allowed to express plenty of negative emotion but the children are disciplined if they react in a negative way to unfair treatment. It's almost like the children are expected to have more self control than the adults are expected to have.

> 2. Always protect someone else, but never yourself. You see this quite often in family systems where there is physical or sexual abuse present. Sometimes really sick behavior continues for generations because no one in the family is willing to expose it for fear of retribution or retaliation.

> 3. Keep the family "secrets" so that no one outside the family will know the truth about what goes on behind closed doors in your home. Often very sick behavior takes place within the family and continues for many years because everyone in the family has been trained to protect certain family members even if it means not protecting others in the family from abusive treatment.

4. Children are to be seen but not heard. This rule often gives the adults license to say and do whatever they wish, and children are often not given a voice.

5. In some families, it is communicated that unlawful behavior or going against societal morals is totally okay...just as long as you don't get caught. Often, you see this in families where the adults are drug addicts, alcoholics or have sexual issues.

JUST FYI

On a lighter note...

I once heard a story about a silly rule that had been carefully passed down through the generations. A young man married a beautiful young woman and was eager to begin living life as a married couple. He loved having roast, carrots and potatoes for Sunday dinner. He noticed, however, that his young bride would cut off both ends of the roast before she put it in the pan to cook. He wondered about why she did it...after all...she was cutting off some good pieces of meat. So...he asked her why she did it. She responded by saying, "that's what my mother always did." So, he took it all in stride until they went to her mother's house one Sunday after church and noticed that his mother in law did the exact same thing. He got up the courage to ask her why she cut off the ends of the roast before she cooked it. His mother in law responded, "That's what my mother always did." Even though he was somewhat perplexed by the practice of cutting off the ends of perfectly good meat, he just let it go. One Easter Sunday they decided to go to his wife's grandmother's house for roast and potatoes. Much to his surprise, the dear old lady did NOT cut off the ends of the roast before she cooked it....she cooked the whole thing! So, he asked her about it. "Granny...my wife (your granddaughter) and my mother in law (your daughter) always cut off the ends of a perfectly good roast when they cook it. When I asked them about it...they said they learned it from you. So why didn't you do it just now?" The old woman looked at him over the rim of her glasses and said, "Honey, the only reason I ever did it in the past was if the roast was too big for the pan!" Here is an example of a silly rule that had been carefully passed down through the generations and no one really knew why. ☺

B. Not all family rules are bad. Some rules are really good and help bring unity and harmony to the family. These are the kind of rules that help the family function and conduct life in an orderly fashion. Rules like, "clean up after yourself", "learn to share with others", "respect other family member's privacy and boundaries" are really good rules to govern family behavior. Teaching children to do things the right way and with excellence will carry over into their own families as they get older. Good rules can actually help families be more productive and can teach children great ways to live life when they grow up and have families of their own.

C. Then, there are moral and true rules that God has laid down for us to live by in the Ten Commandments. If we try to live by these godly rules or boundaries, we will experience more harmony in our relationships with each other. If we live by God's rules, we won't have to worry about harming others or even ourselves and can live our lives in a much healthier and peaceful way.

2. How children learn rules

A. Consistent modeling is the best way to teach children how to obey appropriate rules. Children learn rules when parents lovingly and consistently encourage their children to do things in a right manner. Consistency and modeling produce responsible children. If a child is shown how to do something well and with excellence, it will become something they will strive to do because it feels good to do things the right way and they can get a great deal of satisfaction from the success of their efforts.

B. Children can also learn rules through anxiety. This is not a healthy way for children to learn rules, but they will learn them just the same. Confusion and chaos in the family creates anxiety. Children learn ways of reacting through the chaos. These are usually the unspoken rules of the family. In a dysfunctional family, a child can learn things like, "run and hide when daddy comes home drunk or when mom and dad are arguing". Or…they can learn things like, "don't bother mom when she is in a bad mood." They don't have to have the rule spoken to them verbally in order for them to learn how to react or not react in a given situation. By consistently experiencing negative behavior and reactions in the family, a child will absolutely learn how to read the situation and will know what to do or not do based on what the situation warrants.

C. Children also learn rules through fear of abandonment. Children are destroyed emotionally when parents withhold affection in order to get them to behave. Children should never be abandoned emotionally or in any other way. It is important not to tell your children that you are going to leave them if they don't do what you say. God has promised to never leave us and to never abandon us. His promise is not contingent upon our behavior. We often disobey God because we are human and prone to sinful behavior. We often think that our way is better than His way. Even when we are disobedient, God does not abandon us. He may discipline us and we may experience the pain of our bad choices, but we never have to fear that God will walk away from us because we disappoint Him. We should determine that we will never abandon our children regardless of what they do. Part of teaching them the right way to live is to also teach them the law of sowing and reaping…that there are consequences to bad behavior. But one thing they should always be able to rely on is the fact that we will never stop loving them and will be there to help them when they make a mistake.

D. Parental anxiety teaches children the rules of the family in a negative way. If one or both parents are intense, angry, insecure or mean, their behavior teaches children negative ways to live life.

E. Children also learn rules by consequences. This is actually a principle that God teaches us in His word. There are consequences to our behavior, whether our behavior is good or bad. If we do the right thing, the consequences will be favorable. If we do the wrong thing, there is a really good chance it will come back to bite us. It is the law of sowing and reaping in action. Consistent, loving discipline teaches children that there are boundaries and rules in life and that they must learn to be obedient.

3. The need for closeness and distance

The foundation of personhood is laid in a life between birth and six years of age. If the child's needs are not met during those years, anxiety will become a major problem in the child's life. This anxiety plays out in the formation of insecure boundaries. We become either overly dependent or overly independent when there has been a lack of bonding.

Every child has a need for closeness (togetherness). This closeness will produce a sense of belonging…in other words; we know we belong if we bonded properly in our family of origin.

We need to be able to feel the support of our parents in order to grow in a healthy way. We need to know that we are valuable and unique and that our parents value, affirm and encourage our uniqueness. We also need a strong sense of security and safety.

Of course, it goes without saying that we need unconditional love more than anything else. We need that sense of nurturing and approval. We need guidance and proper correction; however, we need our positive aspects to be the main focus. From time to time, parents will have to point out and correct inappropriate behavior or wrong choices. Yet, if the negative things about the child's behavior or actions are the main focus, the child can become so discouraged they eventually give up and quit trying to do the right thing altogether. If a parent sees and acknowledges the good points more often than the bad points, the child will tend to want to do the right thing more often than the wrong thing.

4. The need for distance (separateness)

As mentioned above, a child really needs the sense of closeness and bonding that come especially in the first six years of life. While bonding is important throughout the individual's life, it is especially vital in those first six years. When a child has bonded properly in the first six years, a natural and healthy sense of separateness will begin when the child is around 7 to 8 years old. When a child begins to show healthy independence, it is a good sign that proper bonding has taken place. By the time a child is around 13 years old that sense of separateness is in full force. Often, parents freak out and worry that something is wrong when a child begins to desire some independence. If a child has properly bonded with the parents, they feel secure in stretching their wings a bit and venturing out because they know who they are, they know who their family is and they know that mom and dad are always there to come to when they need help or encouragement. Independence is not a bad thing when it is the product of good bonding. In fact, independence is a celebration of our uniqueness and separateness from mother.

A child also needs to develop a sense of autonomy (self-rule). Autonomy is when we begin to operate in our freedom of choice. Of course, this must be age appropriate. The best way I can describe it is that when we have properly bonded with our parents, there will be a sense of freedom because we are secure in our parent's love. When we are secure we can separate or draw near without fear of abandonment.

At this point in our development, we will begin to exhibit a strong sense of self-direction. This is when we can begin to set our own goals and have our own dreams.

When a child has properly bonded and has been given the opportunity to develop a strong sense of closeness and separateness, and has been allowed to grow into the realization that they are an individual with unique gifts and talents, the parents won't have to worry about the child's character. A child who has been given the opportunity to develop in a healthy way will not be an individual who gives in to negative peer pressure. The parent won't have to worry about the following:

a. Negative compliance. This is when we want peace at all cost so we don't stand up against negative influence or unhealthy peer pressure. This is a big problem especially among teenagers. However, if proper bonding has taken place in the family of origin and if the parents have given the child the freedom to grow as an individual with good and healthy boundaries that have been clearly communicated and explained, the child will be less likely to rebel.

b. Rebellion is developed when a child is not given the opportunity to understand why healthy rules and boundaries are in place. The whole "Don't do as I do...do as I say" or "Do it just because I said so because I'm the parent" statements often foster rebellion in children. Authority without relationship will often breed rebellion.

JUST FYI

The Truth about Hugs...

Touch is a powerful means of connection. It is said that we need 7 hugs a day for healthy functioning, and 12 hugs a day for healing. Many people are isolated and do not get this important need met. They may not feel comfortable with hugs or appropriate touch because they either didn't experience it in their family of origin or people may have hugged them with wrong motives accompanied by abuse or a demand for something costly in return. We can express God's love for others by offering them a simple, appropriate hug from time to time (with permission of course) and with no strings attached!

---

5. The dramatic triangle: Dysfunctional roles in the family

In a dysfunctional family, the different family members often resort to unhealthy ways of relating. Depending on certain behaviors that have passed down through the generations and have been modeled by grandparents and so forth, the level of dysfunction can cause significant problems in how the members of the family relate to each other. Often, there is one family member who tends to be the most dominant in how they relate to the others. There will also tend to be family members that relate in different ways to the dominant personality. In Theotherapy, we talk about the dramatic triangle…roles that reflect sick ways of relating.

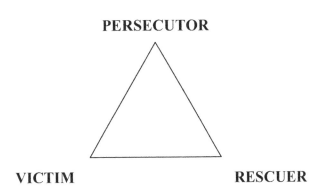

PERSECUTOR

VICTIM   **RESCUER**

A. The persecutor

      1. The persecutor is generally the dominant personality in a dysfunctional family system and will often tend to control the others by bullying, criticizing and getting in the other family member's space. They tend to ignore healthy boundaries and will get the results they desire from others in the family through their anger or obstinacy. A persecutor gains power by being bigger, louder, meaner and more intimidating than anyone else in the relationship.

      2. The persecutor tends to destroy in others what he/she has suppressed in self. They tend to be harder on those in the relationship they fear may reflect their own weaknesses. They have learned over time that they can get what they want if they

are forceful enough or continue to pursue their agenda even if they find out they are wrong.

B. The victim

1. The victim controls by being helpless and needy. When you first think about it, the role of victim may sound weak and powerless. However, the victim is a very powerful role in the dramatic triangle. The victim controls others as well as their own environment by playing on the sympathy of others in the relationship.

2. The victim does not accept responsibility for any dysfunction in the relationship because they see themselves as having no control. If the victim can focus on their neediness instead of their dysfunctional behavior, they don't have to make any changes themselves.

C. The rescuer

1. The rescuer controls by being a "savior" for everyone else in the family. At first glance, you might think the role of rescuer is a noble role...after all...they are always concerned about the underdog. However, the rescuer ultimately believes that God is not in control of the situation and that they are needed to take charge of everything or their world will fall apart. They often develop a secret martyr complex because people do not "appreciate" their efforts.

2. The rescuer often feels guilty when they see others struggling since it is up to the rescuer to fix things. They truly believe that the family would fall apart if they weren't there managing and salvaging everything.

The problem with each of these roles is that they are dysfunctional. They produce a lack of security and boundaries within the family unit. In truth, these roles are rooted in a need to feel in control of the situation. Whether functioning as a persecutor, victim or rescuer, the whole motivation behind the action is fear of not being in control. Fear is at the root of all control.

In a dysfunctional family, different family members will tend to default to a certain role, however, the roles can shift rapidly from one person to the next.

For example: Let's say dad is the persecutor, mom is the victim and the kids are the rescuers. Dad bullies mom to get her to do whatever it is he wants her to do. Mom plays the victim card well in front of the kids and the kids are always coming to her defense. However, when mom has had enough, she fights back and becomes hostile and critical. All of a sudden, the dad is acting like the victim and wonders why everyone is mad at him. Or, the kids get mad at dad for being so tough on mom so they gang up against him with mom. And so on and on it goes with everyone switching roles. The only problem is that all of these roles are nothing more than masks to cover insecurity and fear…thus the need to control…whatever that may look like. Often, the choice of roles in the dramatic triangle is a reflection of the original family role in the parents' families of origin. (*If it worked for me to be a rescuer in my family of origin, it will work for me to be a rescuer in my marriage*).

Believe it or not, an issue can play a role in the dysfunctional family. Things like depression, addiction, illness, etc. can all add to the mix in causing the family to relate in unhealthy ways. We may decide that our addiction or illness is in control of our lives and we act accordingly by allowing it to rule over us with no effort to break free from its dominance in our lives. We begin to break free when we allow God to have the control of our lives.

6. De-triangling

So…once you determine that your family is all messed up in the dramatic triangle, how can you break free from relating in such a dysfunctional way?

A. Believe it or not…when one person in the family respectfully refuses to play their dysfunctional role, the triangle begins to disintegrate. It is impossible to continue to function according to the rules of the dramatic triangle if the persecutor decides to quit persecuting, or the victim decides to quit using their neediness or weakness as a means of control, or the rescuer decides that not every disagreement is their responsibility to fix.

B. Defining participation in the triangle and setting healthy boundaries destroys the triangle. However, you can expect resistance to change. Unhealed people tend to cling to dysfunctional ways of relating if it has become their "normal" or familiar way of relating. They would rather put up with the pain than make the changes necessary to have healthy relationships.

C. When we invite God into the conflict and allow Him to fight our battles or help us through the difficult situation, it absolutely begins to change the way we relate to others in a godlier, healthy way. When we are submitted to God as a family and live our lives according to His principles, there will be unity, harmony and freedom to disagree without feeling the need to control others.

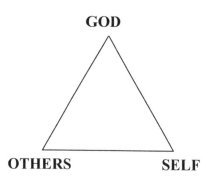

7. The emotionally healthy family

In the emotionally healthy family good communication is vital. An emotionally healthy family allows each person to be who they really are and provides a safe place to learn from their mistakes and still be loved. We cannot have that kind of healthy relationship if there is no effective communication occurring in the family.

A. In an emotionally healthy family, communication is spoken and direct. We often play games with others by thinking they should just "pick up" what we want to communicate solely through our attitudes and body language. People are different. We should not automatically assume that they perceive the situation the same way we do. In an emotionally healthy family, we do not make assumptions that the other family members automatically know what we want. We need to learn to "say what we mean, and mean we say."

B. In an emotionally healthy family, there are no unspecified expectations. Learn to let your needs and wants be known in a straight-forward, honest manner with members of your family. We need to learn to communicate our expectations, instead of hoping the other persons in the family will simply read our mind and act accordingly.

C. In an emotionally healthy family, we identify destructive games and stop playing them.

We need to recognize the dysfunctional things we tend to do to each other within our family unit and make the changes necessary to relate in healthier ways. We must learn to honor and respect each other. There is never a good reason to show disrespect to others. As God works healing into our lives, we will see where we have shown disrespect to others and He will give us the grace and ability to change.

D. In an emotionally healthy family, genuine warmth is expressed. Ask God to teach you how to be warm, loving, and giving. Learn how to show affection to those you love.

E. In an emotionally healthy family, genuine empathy is felt (putting yourself in the other person's shoes). If you do not understand the other members of the family, then they probably will not understand you. It takes a desire to change and a willingness to reach out to the members of your family. It is important to try to see life from the other person's viewpoint. Try to understand their perspective (how they are viewing the situation). Try to get into their world.

F. Genuine interest in one another is expressed. Learn to genuinely care about the people in your family: spouse, children, sisters, brothers, parents, and extended family members. Quality time spent listening to the other person will cause them to feel loved.

G. Behavior outside of family should parallel behavior inside the family. It is important to be the same person you are in public as you are at home. A bad attitude with your spouse carries over into every area of the family. When a husband and wife do not get along, it causes the children to be greatly confused and insecure.

H. More positive expressions of emotion become the norm, not because negative emotions are suppressed, but because they are expressed and resolved in a healthy manner. Emotions are acknowledged, not ignored. Learn how to identify emotions and to feel comfortable with them. Learn to relate properly to other's feelings and emotions. When you are upset, ask yourself the question: *"Am I mad, sad, do I feel embarrassed, etc.?" "What am I feeling right now"?* Learn to identify good feelings as well. In time, your family will start experiencing more positive emotion than negative emotion.

I. In the emotionally healthy family, privacy is respected. Family members need privacy and respect. Show teenagers you have confidence in them by giving them privacy. Every person in the family should be able to have their own space, which will build trust and also instill a respect for other people's boundaries.

J. Every person has the right to be an individual. Children should not be compared to each other or valued based on their performance. Every person's opinion should be welcomed and validated even if disagreed with.

K. Problem solving is a family endeavor. Everyone has the freedom to voice their opinion on how family problems should be resolved.

L. Emotionally healthy families must remain flexible. Children should be taught that flexibility is part of how a healthy family should function, keeping in mind that different personalities adjust to change differently.

M. Children need good parental role models. Parents should model love, respect and acceptance. Children can only reflect what is modeled for them.

N. Emotionally healthy families learn to share pain and be able to sustain loss together. Individual family members will respond differently to pain and loss and each person should be validated in healthy expressions of grief.

O. Children can perceive if their parents are not in harmony sexually, and it will make them insecure. Parents should express appropriate physical touch and romantic interaction with each other in front of the children so that the children feel confident in their parent's love for each other.

P. The family needs to be a safe environment to take risks and to be vulnerable. Parents should encourage children to develop their own likes, hobbies, interests and goals without fear of being compared to others.

Q. Families need to be able to share household responsibilities so that each person feels a part of the family unit. Children should see that they are part of the family "team" regardless of their age.

JUST FYI

Peace-keeper vs. Peace-maker...
Sometimes we confuse being a Peace-maker with being a Peace-keeper. Believe it or not...they are not the same thing. Check this out:

Peace-keeper – A person who complies with the wishes of others simply because they are afraid to have conflict. A peace-keeper keeps peace at all costs even if it means they are not authentic in the process. This is rooted in the fear of man.

Peace-maker – A person who is willing to wade through conflict in order to see it come to a place of resolution, even if the resolution to the conflict is agreeing to disagree agreeably. This is the type of person Jesus referred to in the Sermon on the Mount when He said, *"Blessed are the peacemakers, for they will be called sons of God."* Matthew 5:9

So...what are you? A Peace-keeper or a Peace-maker?

*****READ BEFORE STARTING*****

In order for you to complete the Theotherapy program all Study Questions and the Life Applications Sections must be completed and graded. Facilitators may grade Study Questions. The Life Application section will be reviewed by the group leader ONLY. Please don't hesitate to ask for help if needed!!!

Study Questions

1. Name some ways (both good and bad) that children can learn rules.

2. List the three roles in the dramatic triangle and how each role tries to control their environment.

3. What characteristic of an emotionally healthy family most resonates with you? Why?

4. Compare the difference between a peace-keeper and a peace-maker.

Life Application

1. Can you give an example of a good rule from your family of origin? How has that rule affected you as an adult?

2. Can you give an example of a dysfunctional rule from your family of origin? How has that rule affected you as an adult?

DYNAMICS MODULE #15:

1. Who was there for you (or not there for you) emotionally as a child?

2. What kind of parental role model(s) did you have?

3. Who played what role (persecutor, victim or rescuer) in your family of origin?

4. What role did <u>you</u> play?

MODULE # 16

MARRIAGE

The LORD God said, "It is not good for the man to be alone. I will make a helper suitable for him." Genesis 2:18

At some point in time, we all think about sharing our life with someone. Unless you have been given a special gift of singleness, most of us long to share life, joy, intimacy and companionship with someone we are compatible with in a deeply committed and exclusive relationship. We may spend a great deal of time thinking about certain character traits in others that are appealing to us, physical characteristics that attract us and common goals or dreams that coincide with our own. We want to be happy and fulfilled. So, we set out to find that special someone. For most of us, we generally tend to go through three basic steps in choosing a mate.

Our way...

1. *Physical attraction* - Have you ever walked into a room or into a situation and saw someone across the room that you felt an immediate physical attraction for? We notice their hair, their eyes, the curve of their face, their smile, their body shape and size, the sound of their laughter and we make a mental note of whether or not we would like to get to know them better. We want to be in relationship with someone we feel physically attracted to...after all, everyone likes fireworks...so we begin to pursue that person. If all goes well and the other person is attracted to us too, we may enter into a "relationship". And so it begins...the warm fuzzies...that feeling of desire to be with them constantly, the desire to show them off to our family and friends...they may just be "the one" so we find ourselves well on our way to a committed relationship. If all goes well and we are reasonably compatible, we enter into the next phase of the relationship...the emotional connection.

2. *Emotional connection* – So, now that you have entered into the bliss of finding someone you are physically attracted to...if all goes well and you get along pretty good, then...you "fall in love". Talk about the warm fuzzies! You can't stand being away from them...you think about them all the time...you decide that they are the one for you and hopefully, you both decide to be exclusive in your relationship. Once you figure out that you are physically attracted and emotionally connected, then you may take the next

step and decide to "tie the knot". You plan your wedding, you make all the necessary decisions to get your life ready for living together as husband and wife…and then with all of your friends and family present, you go through the ceremony of holy matrimony. You finally made it! You are married now and you move into all of the benefits of marital bliss. At some point, you may decide to have children and your priorities begin to shift. You start thinking about what it means to be a parent to someone who depends on you for everything. You want them to be trained well and to grow up to be healthy human beings with a good moral compass. If you are a Christian, you may begin to think of important things like having a family that places a priority on spirituality and church. You may decide that raising kids is a very important aspect of life so you make the decision to make Christ the center of your family. At that point, you may have become connected enough with each other to really focus on the spiritual aspect of your relationship. That's when you move into the next phase…the spiritual connection.

3. *Spiritual connection* - Sounds awesome doesn't it? Sounds like a match made in heaven. It can't get much better than this right? Good physical connection…good emotional connection and now the icing on the cake…you are connected spiritually. Most of us would agree that this is the typical way of finding a mate to share life with:

Physical attraction $\longrightarrow$ emotional connection $\longrightarrow$ spiritual connection. All is right with the world!

Would it surprise you to find out that while this may work in many cases, it was not God's plan from the beginning? Did I shock you? By taking a look at Scripture, we can see how God's plan was established and how the fall of mankind through the sin and disobedience of Adam and Eve in the Garden of Eden set mankind on a course for doing things backwards. So, let's compare our way with His way.

God's way…

1. *Spiritual connection* – Marriage and the joining of two people together was God's idea from the beginning. According to Genesis 2:15-25, God saw that Adam (who was created first) was not complete.

The LORD God took the man and put him in the Garden of Eden to work it and take care of it. And the LORD God commanded the man, "You are free to eat from any tree in the garden; but you must not eat from the tree of the knowledge of good and evil, for when you eat from it you will certainly die."

The LORD God said, "It is not good for the man to be alone. I will make a helper suitable for him."

Now the LORD God had formed out of the ground all the wild animals and all the birds in the sky. He brought them to the man to see what he would name them; and whatever the man called each living creature, that was its name. So the man gave names to all the livestock, the birds in the sky and all the wild animals.

But for Adam no suitable helper was found. So the LORD God caused the man to fall into a deep sleep; and while he was sleeping, he took one of the man's ribs and then closed up the place with flesh. Then the LORD God made a woman from the rib he had taken out of the man, and he brought her to the man.

The man said,

"This is now bone of my bones
    and flesh of my flesh;
she shall be called 'woman,'
    for she was taken out of man."

That is why a man leaves his father and mother and is united to his wife, and they become one flesh.

Adam and his wife were both naked, and they felt no shame. Genesis 2:15-25

So get this…it was God who saw that mankind was alone and needed a companion and partner. Adam had no clue that anything was missing in his life. He was going about his business of tending the Garden and naming the animals…nothing was amiss as far as he was concerned…he knew nothing different. So God, in His divine wisdom and love for Adam, decided to not start from scratch in making a partner for him…He decided to take part of Adam's body to form a perfect counterpart for Adam. God causes Adam to get sleepy and lay down for a nap. While he is asleep, God opens Adam up, takes out a rib, closes him back up and forms this unbelievably beautiful creature to join with Adam.

2. *Emotional connection* - When Adam wakes up, God brings Eve to him and then Adam has a very emotional response when he sees this beautiful woman: "You are bone of my bones, flesh of my flesh; I will call you woman because you were taken out of me!" You can't express a deeper emotional response than what Adam made at the moment of meeting Eve for the first time. So, it all began with a spiritual connection (God's idea) and then the spiritual connection brought an emotional response (emotional

connection). The result, the byproduct, the "fruit" of their spiritual and emotional connection was then to join physically.

3. *Physical connection* - Now that Adam and Eve were connected spiritually and emotionally, they demonstrated that spiritual and emotional "oneness" by connecting physically.

Adam made love to his wife Eve and she became pregnant and gave birth to Cain. She said, "With the help of the LORD I have brought forth a man." Later she gave birth to his brother Abel. Genesis 4:1-2

So, according to the Bible, we see that God's plan was exactly the opposite of what became man's normal way of picking a spouse. Here is the comparison:

God's plan: spiritual, then emotional, then physical
vs.
Man's plan: physical, then emotional, then spiritual

Sin always turns things upside down from the way God originally intended it to be. The best marriages are the ones that cultivate spiritual and emotional connection before the physical intimacy takes place. When we lay a foundation built on doing it opposite of God's way, we may have problems once the physical attraction begins to diminish. There's just so much intimacy a purely physical connection can bring to the relationship. It's kind of like putting the cart before the horse. Developing a strong spiritual bond, then experiencing the joy and emotional connection that comes when we find we are in harmony spiritually, will tend to help us build on the things that are truly important in a marriage relationship. The physical connection is very important, it is definitely a part of God's design for fulfillment in the marriage, but it falls short of what the relationship can be if we are trying to build emotionally or spiritually on a foundation built on a purely physical connection.

God is for marriage and for the partnership of a man and woman to accomplish His plan for us and for us to enjoy lifelong intimacy. If marriages are sound in all aspects, spiritual, emotional and physical, we will find that our journey in this life is enhanced and augmented by the person God has put in our life to be our mate.

So why do so many marriages struggle?

1. Most couples have no real or tangible goals for how they want their relationship to grow and to flourish. Not in every case, but in most cases, couples may have certain goals like establishing themselves financially, enjoying the fruit of their labors by having material things that make life easier or more fun, and by making it through the child rearing years with minimal difficulty. However, there are more goals that are needed in a marriage besides financial stability, the accumulation of wealth or possessions and paying for your kids' college. A healthy marriage will have goals in place that see clear and definite growth in the marriage relationship over time. Ask yourself the question: where do I want my marriage to be in five years, ten years and fifty years. What are some things that I can do for my spouse that will help them to feel more loved and cherished as time goes by? Have you noticed that in a lot of marriages, the following scenario is the way people tend to live out the years of their marriage?

Get up
Get the kids fed and off to school
Go to work
Come home
Fix dinner
Get the kids bathed and in bed
Grab some husband and wife time
Go to bed
Get up
Get the kids fed and off to school....and so on...day after day. For some marriages, just surviving the daily routine is about all that is accomplished. The years pass by, the kids grow up and move out and establish their own families, etc. What do we have left to show for the years of toughing it out together and struggling through the storms that life brings? If we want our marriages to get better with time…we need to invest in the relational aspects of our marriage. We need to grow and transform into healthier individuals and couples as the years go by.

Here are some practical things that can help a marriage grow deeper and healthier over time.

a. To have a good marriage, you must learn to die to self. Marriage is hard work. It takes a lot for two different people who are wired differently to learn to give and take in a way that is mutually beneficial for both parties and for the family. If you always have to have things your way or if you always have to be right, someone will be getting the short end of the stick. A good marriage requires a willingness to compromise for the good of your partner.

b. Healthy couples regularly extend forgiveness to each other. Any marriage can be healed from deep pain and disappointment if _both_ partners are willing to work on it. If you have communication problems, personality conflicts, individual struggles and issues and even fail each other, the marriage can make it if repentance and forgiveness are readily extended to each other. I tell people often that my marriage to my wife has been through just about everything a marriage can go through and we have still survived. I have hurt my wife on many occasions over the years and there have been times she has hurt me. Some of the pain and disappointments we have caused each other have been very deep. Yet, if we had given up and not tried to live out the concept of repentance and forgiveness, we would not have seen God work in and through our lives individually and as a couple.

c. Healthy marriages include realistic goals for growth. Some goals in marriage should include the following:

> 1. Find out the needs of your partner and then learn to be aware and considerate of each other's needs. Notice I didn't say learn to _meet_ each other's needs. It is impossible to truly meet the deepest needs in another person's soul. God alone is our "need-meeter" and He is the only one who truly knows every intimate aspect of our background, our fears and internal conflicts and what we need to become more healthy human beings. I will never be able to meet the deepest needs of my wife's soul and she can never meet mine. That is God's department. However, I can learn to be sensitive to my spouse's needs and I can let her know that I am with her, on her side and cherishing her every step of the way. My wife can't meet my deepest needs...but she can be aware of the things I need in order to feel loved, listened to and cherished.

> 2. One of the things that make us different as men and women is that men generally need their egos to be built up and women generally need to have their emotions validated. I have often shared in Theotherapy that most reasonably emotionally healthy men can accomplish just about anything...can climb any

mountain and fight any battle if they believe their wife thinks they are a good husband, father, lover and provider. Most reasonably healthy women can fight any battle and overcome any obstacle if they believe their husband hears them, sees them and validates how they feel. It's how God wired us. When we treat our spouse like they are supposed to be just like us in every way, we miss the enjoyment of stepping outside of our comfort zone to build them up and to enhance their happiness. Learning how to genuinely encourage and build one another up is an important goal in marriage as well as learning how to understand and validate someone who might see things differently than I do. Both partners should treat each other with mutual respect.

3. Another goal in marriage should be to learn to stop manipulating in order to get our own needs met. We manipulate others when we feel insecure or have low self-esteem. Learning to communicate with each other in a direct, honest and loving way enhances intimacy.

4. We can learn to enhance communication by saying what we mean and meaning what we say. In Theotherapy we talk about listening with the "third ear". That basically means learning to listen to their heart, not just their words, and finding out what they are really trying to communicate to us even though their words or attitudes may not reflect the real heart behind what they are saying.

5. Often we try to change the other person in the relationship to make us feel safer and more in control of the situation, especially if we are fearful. A good goal in marriage should be to stop trying to change the other person. Work on changing yourself. God will change the other person in His time. In the meantime, focus on your issues and on your relationship with God. If you are dealing with your issues and pressing into intimate relationship with God, you won't have time to tweak or control the other person. Be authentic in your communication, let your needs and wants be known in a straightforward and honest manner, but give God the opportunity to deal with your spouse if he/she has issues that need to be changed. If you try to change them, you will most

likely end up with more resistance and frustration than anything else.

6. Interrupt destructive cycles of behavior. There are certain things that make marriage more difficult and breed more conflict. Get rid of old habits, attitudes and relationships that continue to get you into trouble or foster conflict within the marriage. We aren't in the marriage just for us and what we need...we are in it to partner with someone in living life to the fullest. Stop going to places and hanging out with people who continue to pull you away from God and from the relationships that really matter.

7. Identify areas where growth/change must occur in your own life. A good goal in marriage is to seek to improve yourself in as many ways as possible. The healthier you are emotionally, the healthier your marriage will tend to be especially if your spouse is working on themselves in the same way.

8. Negotiate and implement a workable and realistic plan for nurturing the marriage. A workable plan could include things like:

> a. Each person must be responsible for their own reactions and feelings. I am not responsible for my partner's reactions or feelings.

> b. Identify strategies for logistical changes in the relationship realizing that every person is responsible for changing themselves. You cannot effectively change each other. Which is better...to always be right or to have a good relationship? When you are emotionally healthy, you don't always have to be right nor do you always have to be wrong. A truly authentic person can own their strengths and weaknesses equally because neither defines them as a human being nor do our strengths and weaknesses determine our value and worth to God.

9. Arouse realistic hope that things can always get better. Remember this...as much as you want your marriage to be

healthy and to work, God wants it more. The following Scripture reflects God's heart for us and for our marriages:

"For I know the plans I have for you, "declares the Lord, "plans to prosper you and not to harm you, plans to give you hope and a future. Then you will call upon me and come and pray to me, and I will listen to you." Jeremiah 29:11, 12

10. A really good goal in marriage is to establish family meetings. Meet on a regular basis so that all in the family have an opportunity to talk about what is going on in the marriage relationship or family (children included but age appropriate discussions of course).

    a. Asking questions like: What has changed in our family dynamic? What still needs to change and what can we do better as a family or as a marriage partnership?

    b. How do we implement the needed changes?

    c. What are some realistic and attainable goals for our family?

In summary, marriage can be difficult at times but it is the way God designed for us to share life with another person and to accomplish great things in the time we have on this earth. We might experience some very painful things in marriage…things like communication problems, strong differences of opinion, infidelity, financial struggles, illness, death of a family member and so on. However, if we are committed to growing and maturing as an individual and as a couple…and if we are determined to repent when we have failed and to extend forgiveness when others fail us…we can be well on our way to enjoying the marriage relationship the way God intended from the beginning.

In order for you to complete the Theotherapy program all Study Questions and the Life Applications Sections must be completed and graded. Facilitators may grade Study Questions. The Life Application section will be reviewed by the group leader ONLY. Please don't hesitate to ask for help if needed!!!

Study Questions

1. Contrast society's way of choosing a mate versus God's plan for the same thing.

2. Healthy marriages include realistic goals for growth. List three realistic goals from what you read in this chapter.

Life Application

1. In your own words, write down what you think an emotionally healthy marriage should look like.

2. List some goals you have for your own marriage or if you are not married, goals you would like to have if you did get married.

MODULE # 17

DIVORCE

We live in a time and culture where half of all marriages end in divorce. Practically all of us have been touched in some way by divorce. Whether we personally have experienced divorce from someone we were married to, or experienced the ripple effect of divorce as collateral damage in someone else's divorce, we all know the devastation that a divorce can bring. It is impossible for a divorce to only affect the couple who have decided to part ways. It affects children, extended family members, close friends and acquaintances. Divorce has been called "the death of a marriage."

JUST FYI

Looking at the residual effects of divorce…

Years ago I worked for a sign company and one of the production techniques we used was to laminate (bond together with very strong glue) two sheets of plywood in order to cut sign letters from the double thick wood. The two sheets of plywood effectively became "one" sheet or piece. If someone decided to try to pry the two sheets of wood apart, it was impossible to do so without destroying the two pieces of wood. Invariably, fragments and splinters from one piece would still be stuck to the other sheet of plywood even though the two pieces had been separated. The same thing is true about a marriage covenant that is torn apart…it leaves pieces of the other person's personality, emotions and "soul" stuck to both individuals. It is impossible to go through a divorce unaffected.

---

1. Divorce is an insult to the ego (soul). When a couple goes through a divorce (at some point before, during or after the decision to part ways), both individuals may feel that what they had to give just wasn't enough. At some point in their history together, they had decided it would be a good idea to marry…otherwise, they would never have said "I do" in the first place. Maybe they had hopes that the other person would make all their dreams come true, or somehow complete them…or bring them incredible joy and happiness. And now…the bottom has fallen out, the person they married has betrayed them, disappointed them or has been untrustworthy. Maybe they just can't get along or find themselves to be

"incompatible" with the other person. What a disaster! We failed! So, a decision is made to part ways once and for all. All of the hopes and dreams come crashing down and each person, even if they are justifiably angry, still have a feeling that somehow they just didn't have what it took to make a good marriage. Of course there is almost always a blame game that ensues. Neither person in the disintegrating marriage wants to own their personal responsibility for the demise of the marriage. But deep down, even if one person was not directly the cause of the breakup, both partners struggle with feeling that somewhere along the line they failed at something…otherwise the marriage would have made it over the long haul.

2. Divorce diminishes self-esteem. It is an attack against who we are which makes us feel inadequate or worthless. We would all like to think that we are emotionally healthy enough, morally sound enough and thoroughly devoted enough to succeed in marriage. Yet, when we find ourselves in a failed marriage, we begin to realize that maybe we didn't have what it takes to succeed. That hurts.

3. Divorce creates guilt. We may struggle with questions like: *"What could I have done differently?"* *"If only I would have been different…then maybe we would still be together"*. or…. *"What is wrong with me? I must be bad or undesirable."* We may actually be guilty of breaking our marriage vow or of being hard to deal with. In a case where we have actually done something to devastate the marriage, we will experience existential guilt, which we should feel as a result of doing something wrong. But along with existential or real guilt as a result of wrongdoing, we may also struggle with neurotic guilt which is shame based and has to do with who we are versus what we do.

4. Divorce causes a deep sense of personal failure. Often women feel responsible for the relationship. If she can just be a good enough wife, partner, lover, mother, homemaker, etc., then all should be well. But if she finds herself in a failed marriage regardless of the reason, she may be prone to feelings of guilt because she couldn't keep the marriage together, or she wasn't interesting enough or desirable enough to keep her husband's love, affection and attention. For men, divorce is an affront to their ego. All reasonably emotionally healthy men are pretty content if they believe their wife sees them as a good husband, father, lover and provider. When they fail at some or all of the above, they view the divorce as their personal failure.

5. Many times, a divorced person is judged by others. Friends and family wonder why it happened, and sometimes formulate their own version of the events leading up to the divorce. Sometimes they will even choose sides or pick up an offense against one of the divorcing parties based on limited knowledge of the actual situation. Divorces divide families and even destroy long term friendships.

6. Sometimes even the church or faith community may judge the divorcing couple or even choose sides. In years past, the church tended to judge and offered little or no help to the individuals going through the divorce. People were actually ostracized or shunned by some congregations if a couple divorced and neither person was allowed to serve in any capacity in the church. Things have changed in recent years and many churches now offer divorce recovery groups and "newly single" ministries/care groups for divorced persons. God's heart is to heal and restore what has been broken and lost in His people. The church should help restore the broken people who have gone through divorce.

7. When a couple divorces, each person will have feelings that need to be acknowledged and resolved. Some of those feelings that need to be resolved are: anger, bitterness, resentment, loneliness, self-doubt, depression, feelings of abandonment and rejection.

DIFFUSING GRIEF IN DIVORCE

1. Once the marriage has ended or is in the process of ending, both parties will experience some emotions that need to be expressed in a safe environment. As we mentioned before, divorce is basically the death of a marriage. In Part 1 (Healing Me) of this curriculum, we talked about the necessity of learning to effectively grieve our losses. Any loss causes pain, and big losses produce big pain! If someone we love dies, we will experience emotions like shock, anger, sadness, bargaining and eventually resolution. The same thing needs to happen with the loss of a marriage. Something that once upon a time may have seemed wonderful, beautiful and good...turned into something disappointing, devastating and broken. It is very important that each person processes through their pain and anger at the other person and resolves it through genuine forgiveness. If we don't resolve it, we will carry that emotional baggage around with us and maybe drag it

into another relationship. When experiencing the pain of divorce, it is important to get help as quickly as possible before resentment, bitterness and anger build up.

2. In order not to carry excess baggage into a new marriage, it is best to refrain from remarriage until:

a. Major conflicts are resolved. If you do not resolve your own conflicts and internal issues, you will carry them into your next relationship. Not only will you have "junk" from your past relationship...you will invariably at some point come into conflict with "junk" in your new relationship. No one is perfect and everyone has issues. It is naïve to think that you can find a deep relationship anywhere that is free from conflict. So if you don't want to have junk piled on top of more junk...resolve your major emotional conflicts before you enter into a new marriage

b. The vacuum is filled with Christ. Remember, Christ alone can meet the deepest needs of our soul. If we think that some other person has what we need to find complete fulfillment and peace, we are fooling ourselves. When we begin to see God as our "need-meeter", we can enter into deep and loving relationships without the expectation that the other person will somehow fix us or make up for all of the pain from the past. Putting God in the role of meeting our needs and letting the other person off the hook regarding that need actually sets us free to love and be loved, to forgive and be forgiven, to understand and be understood. When we know who we are in Christ, we can have deep and meaningful relationships but those relationships will not define who we are nor will they determine our sense of worth and significance.

c. Faith is restored. The sad reality is that people often experience a crisis of faith when they have lost something as important as a marriage. We may have prayed for God to "fix" our marriage and we may have had other people pray that the marriage would be salvaged. When it doesn't happen, we can be pretty discouraged and even begin to feel that God has somehow let us down. It is human nature to want to have a "go to person" who we believe has the power to make it all better. Unfortunately, we live in a real world where people make bad choices and God will not force His will on any of us to "make us" do the right thing. The Bible tells us that the testing of our faith develops endurance:

"Consider it pure joy, my brothers and sisters, whenever you face trials of many kinds, because you know that the testing of your faith produces perseverance. Let perseverance finish its work so that you may be mature and complete, not lacking anything." James 1:2-4 NIV

d. No demands involving unmet needs remain. Remember, if you begin to think that someone new will meet the deepest needs of your soul, you are fooling yourself at best. If you don't resolve those issues, you will come into a new marriage or relationship expecting the new person to make up for what your former partner didn't give you. That just sets the new marriage or relationship up for failure as well.

e. Resentment toward "ex" is resolved. Ending the marriage is hard enough on everyone involved. You and your former spouse hurt, your kids hurt and family and friends hurt over the loss. Finding the power to forgive the other person truly sets us free to pick up the pieces with God's help and move on with our lives...and helps us be at peace if we have to interact with a former spouse concerning any children from the marriage. You may have even become friends/family with your former in-laws. There is no reason to have to annihilate other relationships simply because you are harboring resentment for someone.

3. Identify and resolve negative patterns from the past that have caused you to get into trouble so you do not repeat the same patterns in your next relationship. The reality is that often the same things that sabotaged the first marriage will sabotage the second if we don't stop negative patterns or behaviors. We need to learn from our mistakes and make every effort to avoid the snares and choices that sabotage our relationships.

4. Accept being single, if applicable. Avoid getting into new relationships "on the rebound". Take time to heal, to think, to deal with your own "frogs and lizards" and to find contentment in the simplicity of being on your own for awhile. It's in those alone times that we may find a great deal of healing and a surge in our spiritual growth and relationship with God. Allow God to bring a new person into your life when He thinks you are ready. You can't go wrong doing it His way.

5. Minimize emotional damage to any children affected by the situation. Make every effort to protect them as much as possible from the emotional "fallout" of the divorce. Do not use them as scapegoats.

a. Emphasize to the children exactly "who" is divorced. It is mommy and daddy who are divorcing...not the children. Assure the children of love from both parents. We really make a serious mistake if we try to use children as pawns to get at our ex. We may feel like we have won a battle but the end result will be long term devastation to the children. It is important for both parents to reinforce the love and commitment of the other parent to the children.

b. Encourage the children to express their anger, anxiety and guilt over the breakup of the marriage. Believe it or not, children often blame themselves for the divorce. It is important not to say "don't feel that way" which invalidates their need to express negative emotion concerning the breakup of their family. They feel what they feel. Rather, ask them to describe how they feel and help them to forgive, encourage them to talk to God about their feelings, talk to a counselor if needed and find peace in knowing that God sees them and understands their pain. Encourage them to develop faith in God who is the perfect parent.

*****READ BEFORE STARTING*****

In order for you to complete the Theotherapy program all Study Questions and the Life Applications Sections must be completed and graded. Facilitators may grade Study Questions. The Life Application section will be reviewed by the group leader ONLY. Please don't hesitate to ask for help if needed!!!

Study Questions:

1. How does divorce diminish self-esteem?

2. What are some common attitudes of the church towards divorce?

3. Why is it a dangerous choice to remarry without having grieved a divorce?

4. How can identifying and resolving patterns from the past help?

5. Name one way to minimize emotional damage to children.

DYNAMICS MODULE #17:

1. How can I become a better spouse? What are some things I need to change and what things do I need to become better at?

2. How can I become a better POTENTIAL spouse? What are some things I need to work on so I don't bring emotional baggage to my future marriage?

MODULE # 18

DISMANTLING STRONGHOLDS/ BREAKING THE CHAINS THAT BIND

Deliverance – *the action of being rescued or set free; a formal or authoritative utterance.*

"Demons dwell in the structures of unforgiveness." Francis Frangipane

Often, our involvement in certain things over the course of our lives can have deep spiritual implications. Whether we were a willing participant or not, sometimes the things we experience open a door to the spiritual realm by creating a "stronghold" or place of bondage to a particular sin or thought pattern. The enemy (Satan) uses the wounds in our lives to establish strongholds of pain, depression, feelings of failure, sinful behaviors and fear.

Stronghold - *a place that has been fortified so as to protect it against attack. A place where a particular cause or belief is strongly defended or upheld.*

Deliverance is sometimes needed to dismantle or uproot a spiritual or mental stronghold that has been established in an individual's life. What can create the need for deliverance? Sin - the enemy dwells in darkness. Every unconfessed sin is a dark place where he could potentially reside.

1. Heredity: Generational curses can cause great struggles in your life. Family sins, struggles and addictions will be passed from generation to generation until someone stops it by repenting.

   "...I, the LORD your God, am a jealous God, punishing the children for the sin of the fathers to the third and fourth generation of those who hate me..." Exodus 20:5

2. Abuse or neglect that creates trauma and places of unresolved hurt and pain are vulnerable to the enemy's attacks.

3. Inner vows or personal decisions: *"I will never..."* Our inner vows hinder God's work in our lives and keep us from being able to

experience freedom in that particular area, enabling the enemy (Satan) to have control over that part of us.

4. Satan is a legalist and delights in holding us to our inner vows, especially if he can keep us in bondage because of them. Jesus called Satan *"Beelzebub"* - *the lord of the flies* in order to communicate how Satan and his demons swarm around wounded, dark places in our lives and establish strongholds of sin, sickness and false beliefs.

5. When this happens, sometimes deliverance is needed in order to completely uproot and remove the demonic oppression from that area of our life.

When should deliverance be performed?

1. As the Holy Spirit leads, not just because it appears to be a good idea. Deliverance can be damaging and do more harm than good, if the person is not ready to fully cease their cooperation with the bondage. It is very important not to administer it apart from the Lord's leading.

2. When the root or creation of the problem has been uncovered. What has caused it? If it is heredity, you may have been cooperating with it without even being aware of it. In order for deliverance to be lasting, the root of the problem must be dealt with. *(How did the enemy gain access?)* Once the root is exposed, as an act of our will, we must choose not to participate in that behavior again.

3. When you are ready and willing to confess whatever part you have played in cooperating with the bondage. If we only want to get rid of the emotional (or spiritual) pain, but do not really want to let go of the sin, then the deliverance will not be lasting.

4. You must grieve the losses you have sustained as a result of your past bondage. You must put to death the idea that you can go back and change the situation or the history of it, or that someone owes you something.

5. If you have not properly grieved a loss, or surrendered your will to God in any area, then deliverance is counterproductive and may result

in having to do deliverance more than once. To avoid this, do not do deliverance until the proper conflicts are resolved. **WHEN IN DOUBT...DON'T.** God is in control and He will set the captives free.

What is the goal of deliverance?

1. To free us so that we can begin to allow the Lord to bring us into Christ-likeness. Being "Christ-like" is <u>not</u> being more religious, it is being freer in allowing God to be central in all aspects of our lives. To be Christ-like is to love others, to walk in obedience to God's will and to choose to walk in forgiveness.

2. To direct the focus our lives on God, instead of being tormented and accused by the lies swimming in our heads. When we know the truth…it sets us free!

3. To free our will to be able to choose God's way so that we will not go back into bondage.

*****READ BEFORE STARTING*****

In order for you to complete the Theotherapy program all Study Questions and the Life Applications Sections must be completed and graded. Facilitators may grade Study Questions. The Life Application section will be reviewed by the group leader ONLY. Please don't hesitate to ask for help if needed!!!

Study Questions

1. When can deliverance be a bad idea?
2. What are some of the conditions necessary for deliverance to be effective?

Life Application

1. Do you see any need for deliverance in your life?
2. If yes, in what areas?

DYNAMICS MODULE #18:

1. Write a letter to Jesus and ask the Holy Spirit to show you any areas of unconfessed sin in your life.

2. What losses have you not completely grieved that are preventing you from reaching *Theotherapeutic* forgiveness?

MODULE # 19

BEYOND HEALING TO MATURITY.

What comes after healing?

1. We all like the idea of being "pain-free" or at least having less and less pain to deal with. Often, when people come to Theotherapy, it is because of great emotional pain in their lives. Pain is a great motivator and it can push us to do or try a variety of things just to make the pain go away. Often, the things we choose in order to "make the pain go away" are addictive, unhealthy or neurotic. In the Theotherapy context, healing itself is not the ultimate goal even though emotional healing is a very good thing to experience. Actually, emotional healing is the highway to get us where we ultimately want to end up…a place called emotional and spiritual maturity. On our healing journey, we must proceed to develop a Christian character that is the natural byproduct or fruit of that healing.

    a.   Paul expressed it this way in Philippians 3:12 (NIV):
"Not that I have already obtained all this, or have already been made perfect, but I press on to take hold of that for which Christ Jesus took hold of me."

    b.   The true goal of every person who is undergoing healing is to proceed to develop his/her character to be more like Jesus.

    c.   The real foundation of such character is love:

        1.   Love for God

        2.   Love for others

        3.   Love for self

    d.   We need to understand and emphasize that this kind of love is of the Holy Spirit, not something we can manufacture ourselves.

2. On our healing journey, we continue to move towards recovery, that is, the restoration of our souls.

    a. Recovery must be looked at as an ongoing process. Philippians 3:12 clearly points this out. In this process we begin to look more and more like Jesus.

    b. Maturity manifests itself through a high level of tolerance for frustration, and through loving what was once unlovable. The more healing we get, the more we understand the need for others to heal and the more we can sympathize and empathize with their journey. Becoming emotionally mature actually makes us less critical of others' issues and motivates us to offer encouragement and support rather than judgment and rejection.

    c. Love is the basic foundation for Christian character. Always remember that love leads us to wholesome character. Love is that which leads us further into maturity.

    d. It is as the infant senses the unconditional love of significant adults that he develops a sense of security. That's why bonding in our family of origin is so important. A sense of safety is a natural byproduct of good and healthy bonding. The more emotionally healed we are, the safer we become to those who encounter us.

    e. A wounded person receives healing through Theotherapy (God's healing) and then must move on to become the kind of Christian person God wants...not because of being more religious...but simply because we want to be like Him.

3. How is this growth accomplished?

    a. As the person is deeply embedded in the word of God, his faith in Jesus Christ becomes strengthened and his love for God, others and self becomes more real. Bonding to God at a deeper level causes us to grow. It's like Jesus said in the Gospel of John:

132

"I am the true vine, and my Father is the gardener. He cuts off every branch in me that bears no fruit, while every branch that does bear fruit he prunes so that it will be even more fruitful. You are already clean because of the word I have spoken to you. Remain in me, as I also remain in you. No branch can bear fruit by itself; it must remain in the vine. Neither can you bear fruit unless you remain in me.

"I am the vine; you are the branches. If you remain in me and I in you, you will bear much fruit; apart from me you can do nothing. If you do not remain in me, you are like a branch that is thrown away and withers; such branches are picked up, thrown into the fire and burned. If you remain in me and my words remain in you, ask whatever you wish, and it will be done for you. This is to my Father's glory, that you bear much fruit, showing yourselves to be my disciples.

"As the Father has loved me, so have I loved you. Now remain in my love. If you keep my commands, you will remain in my love, just as I have kept my Father's commands and remain in his love. I have told you this so that my joy may be in you and that your joy may be complete. My command is this: Love each other as I have loved you. Greater love has no one than this: to lay down one's life for one's friends. You are my friends if you do what I command. I no longer call you servants, because a servant does not know his master's business. Instead, I have called you friends, for everything that I learned from my Father I have made known to you. You did not choose me, but I chose you and appointed you so that you might go and bear fruit—fruit that will last—and so that whatever you ask in my name the Father will give you. This is my command: Love each other. John 15:1-17 NIV

      b.   We must distinguish between developmental stages and maturity. They are two different concepts. All of us go through different stages physically as well as emotionally:

1. baby-hood
2. infancy
3. childhood
4. pre-adolescence
5. young adulthood
6. adulthood, etc.

    c. Rev. Mario Rivera Mendez has said, *"Maturity is the development of good judgment and prudence. Thus a five-year-old may be a mature five-year-old as well as a twenty-one-year-old may be an immature twenty-one-year-old."*

The above section of this lesson was from edited notes by Dr Mario Rivera Mendez.

Walking in maturity: healing is not the goal

When we have been deeply wounded, we will not know who we were designed to be. That is why we must embrace own journey of healing.

"Blessed are those whose strength is in you [Lord], who have set their hearts on pilgrimage. As they pass through the Valley of Baca (weeping), they make it a place of springs; the autumn rains also cover it with pools (blessings). They go from strength to strength until each appears before God in Zion." Psalm 84:5-7NIV

1. Healing is a lifelong process.

    a. We will go from strength to strength. This means that we will often find ourselves getting a significant measure of healing and then later, as we have walked out the new place of healing…God will reveal an even deeper place we need to go to in the next step of our healing journey. It is an ongoing process and we can actually become stronger and more mature as we allow the healing process to accomplish its work in our lives.

    b. In the Old Testament, the children of Israel ran the enemy out of the Promised Land little by little so that they could be strong enough to maintain their victory and keep the wild beasts out. It was a process and involved a continued commitment. God told them to "occupy". It is important to "occupy" our place of healing. That means we continue to cultivate our healing and maintain it by making the right choices, feeding our souls on the right things and pursuing intimacy with God and with others who are mature emotionally and spiritually. If we get some healing, but then do not maintain the boundaries for ourselves that go along with that healing, we can find ourselves slipping back into old, neurotic behaviors.

    c. In the world we will have tribulation…that goes with the territory. Learning to embrace tribulation as a part of healing

(Valley of Baca or "weeping") is a healthy and mature response to processing through our deep wounds and traumas.

2. We must remember that just getting rid of the pain is not the goal either. As I mentioned at the beginning of this module...we all want to be free from pain. But sometimes emotional pain is what motivates us to delve deeper into our issues and find out why we have the pain in the first place.

   a. The Lord by His mercy allows the pain to be there so that we look to Him for help. Pain in our physical body alerts us to a possible problem, an infection or an illness that needs to be addressed and treated. If it weren't for pain, we never would take care of ourselves physically or emotionally. So, God allows pain into our lives to alert us of a problem in our belief system, to motivate us to get healing and to keep us focused on what is truly important...resolving emotional pain and coming to a place of obedience and maturity.

"During the days of Jesus' life on earth, he offered up prayers and petitions with fervent cries and tears to the one who could save him from death, and he was heard because of his reverent submission. Son though he was, he learned obedience from what he suffered and, once made perfect, he became the source of eternal salvation for all who obey him." Hebrews 5:7-9 NIV

   b. We learn obedience through the things we suffer. (Hebrews 5:8 says that about Jesus Christ's own example of suffering.)

The goal is to be like Jesus

1. Bottom line, the ultimate goal of our emotional healing is not freedom from pain, but the development of Christian character.

   a. In order to come to a place of healthy Christian character, the ego must be strengthened in order to be replaced. When a person first comes to Theotherapy, they are often in a place where their life is out of control. Their issues, addictions and faulty belief systems rule their lives. They may be a person who really loves God and wants Him to be on "the throne of their life", but the lies in their belief system scream much louder than the truth of God's Word that sets them free. So, they remain in a place of being out of control, hating every moment of their dysfunctional life, but have no way of breaking the cycle of dysfunction. In order to be at peace and have someone in charge of our lives that clearly has our best interest at heart, we must come to a place of realizing that God needs to be the One in charge. It's like John the Baptist said about Jesus… *"He must increase, but I must decrease."* (John 3:30, NIV). I like the illustration Dr. Mario Rivera uses about how the ego is strengthened in order to replace it:

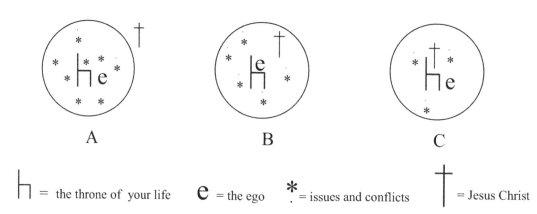

A   B   C

⊢ = the throne of your life   e = the ego   * = issues and conflicts   † = Jesus Christ

*In **A** above, a person initially comes to Theotherapy because they are in a great deal of emotional pain. Their addictions, conflicts and issues are in control (or on the throne of) their life. They may love God and have a relationship with Him, but they keep Him on the outside of their pain because they can't really trust that He has their best interest at heart. In Theotherapy, our job is to help the person become safe enough to explore their issues and to find healing in God.*

*In **B**, we strengthen the person's ego for a time so that they can regain control of their life instead of their issues controlling them. When you offer a safe place for people to process their pain, they will eventually get to the core of their conflicts and issues. For a time, it all becomes about them and we accept and validate them regardless of what they have experienced or done. In the process of helping the person deal with their pain, we help them invite Jesus into their place of pain. Before, they may have been too afraid to ask Him into* *their pain...but as their ego is strengthened and they resolve some of their issues, they feel more power to bring God into their situation.*

In **C**, *the person in need has received enough healing to make their own choice to invite Jesus to be in control of their life. So, they make the choice to relinquish the throne and put Jesus there instead. Their issues and conflicts no longer dominate their life because they have resolved some of them and can trust God to help them resolve even more. It is emotional healing in action!*

b. Abiding in Jesus (bonding to Jesus) produces fruit that remains:

> *"You did not choose me, but I chose you and appointed you so that you might go and bear fruit—fruit that will last—and so that whatever you ask in my name the Father will give you." John 15:16 NIV*

2. Another goal of our emotional healing is so that we may fulfill the greatest commandment:

> *Jesus replied: "'Love the Lord your God with all your heart and with all your soul and with all your mind.' This is the first and greatest commandment. And the second is like it: 'Love your neighbor as yourself.' Matthew 22:37-39*

a. Loving God

   1. Loving God means not serving idols.
      As we mature we will see God and ourselves more clearly. By His grace the Lord reveals Himself and He reveals the idols that we have served (parents, fear, anything that stands between us and God), allowing us to repent.

   2. Those who are forgiven much love much. We love Him because He first loved <u>us</u>. (see Luke 7:47; 1 John 4:19)

137

b. Loving our neighbor

    1. Loving our neighbor is a natural response as we allow God to reveal and heal our places of wounding.

    2. We can give what we have received. When we have received deep emotional healing, we can help others find healing as well.

    3. We seek the highest good of others.

c. Loving self

To love ourselves correctly we must see ourselves as God sees us: as His child, His bride and as His friend

1. We know that we are loved by Him; however, we are dust:

"As a father has compassion on his children, so the LORD has compassion on those who fear him; for he knows how we are formed, he remembers that we are dust." Psalm 103:13,14 NIV

    a. When we know we are loved unconditionally, we are not threatened.

    b. When we know we are loved unconditionally, it frees us to be able to give and receive.

    c. Loving ourselves rightly is a true mark of maturity.

3. Learning to love unconditionally is a byproduct of deep emotional healing. What is real love (*agape*)? (See 1 Corinthians 13)

    a. Love is patient.
    b. Love is kind.
    c. Love does not envy.
    d. Love does not boast.
    e. Love is not proud.

f. Love is not rude.
g. Love is not self-seeking.
h. Love is not easily angered.
i. Love keeps no record of wrongs.
j. Love does not delight in evil but rejoices in the truth.
k. Love always protects.
l. Love always trusts.
m. Love always perseveres.
n. Love never fails.

MATURITY IS THE INTEGRATION OF SPIRIT, SOUL AND BODY.

*****READ BEFORE STARTING*****

In order for you to complete the Theotherapy program all Study Questions and the Life Applications Sections must be completed and graded. Facilitators may grade Study Questions. The Life Application section will be reviewed by the group leader ONLY. Please don't hesitate to ask for help if needed!!!

Study Questions

1. What does it mean to you to develop the character of Christ?

2. What is the goal of healing?

Life Application

1. What would maturity look like in your life?

DYNAMICS MODULE # 19:

1. In what area(s) do you not feel you are walking like Jesus?

Made in the USA
Monee, IL
19 July 2021